SYDNEY GRAY

Brave and Prepared: Elevate Your Interview Game

Transforming Anxiety into Empowerment in Every Job Encounter

Copyright © 2024 by Sydney Gray

All rights reserved. No part of this publication may be reproduced, stored or transmitted in any form or by any means, electronic, mechanical, photocopying, recording, scanning, or otherwise without written permission from the publisher. It is illegal to copy this book, post it to a website, or distribute it by any other means without permission.

First edition

This book was professionally typeset on Reedsy. Find out more at reedsy.com

Contents

Introduction	1
Chapter 1: Understanding the Interview Mindset	6
Chapter 2: Preparation is Key: Researching the Company and...	14
Chapter 3: Mastering Your Personal Pitch	24
Chapter 4: Anticipating Common Interview Questions	33
Chapter 5: Navigating Difficult Questions with Confidence	44
Chapter 6: The Body Language of Confidence	53
Chapter 7: Building Rapport with Your Interviewer	62
Chapter 8: Overcoming Anxiety During the Interview	70
Chapter 9: Managing Virtual Interviews with Confidence	79
Chapter 10: Handling Group and Panel Interviews	88
Chapter 11: Answering Behavioral Questions with Impact	96
Chapter 12: Demonstrating Leadership and Teamwork	105
Chapter 13: Closing the Interview with Confidence	114
Chapter 14: Dealing with Rejection and Moving Forward	123
Chapter 15: Maintaining Confidence Between Interviews	133
Conclusion	143

Introduction

Why Interviews Are More Than Just Q&A

When people think of interviews, they often imagine a straightforward question-and-answer session. The interviewer asks, and the candidate answers—simple, right? Not quite. The truth is, interviews are far more complex. They are dynamic interactions, multifaceted experiences that test more than just your knowledge of the role you're applying for. In reality, interviews are an assessment of your personality, emotional intelligence, adaptability, and even your ability to think on your feet. They are also a conversation where both parties—employer and candidate—are trying to determine whether they are a good fit for each other.

In this sense, interviews should be viewed as two-way streets. While interviewers are trying to assess whether your skills and experience align with the job requirements, you're equally evaluating the company, the culture, and whether the position aligns with your personal and professional goals. This mutual evaluation makes interviews a lot more nuanced than a simple Q&A session. Both you and the interviewer are making choices about your future, and that is a weighty responsibility.

Think of interviews as negotiations or strategic discussions. Your answers should demonstrate your capabilities, but your presence, behavior, and communication skills should also subtly convey your readiness for the role. Body language, how you handle unexpected questions, and how well you manage stress—all contribute to the overall picture you present. Likewise, the questions you ask about the role or the company also speak volumes about your interest, preparation, and thoughtfulness.

Moreover, interviews offer a glimpse into the working environment. Through this exchange, you can evaluate whether the company's values align with yours. Are the interviewers engaging and respectful? Do they seem enthusiastic about the role and the company, or are they mechanical in their questions? These are clues to the company culture. Ultimately, interviews are about more than just exchanging information—they're about building relationships and making a mutual decision on whether to work together.

Transforming Anxiety into Confidence

For most people, the word "interview" conjures feelings of dread, stress, or nervousness. It's a common response—after all, you're being judged and evaluated, often in a very short amount of time. Your future can seem to depend on this one interaction, and the pressure to "get it right" can feel overwhelming. However, anxiety doesn't have to be your enemy. In fact, when harnessed correctly, it can become a tool that helps propel you forward. It's entirely possible to transform your anxiety into confidence, turning what seems like a hurdle into an advantage.

First, it's important to understand that nervousness stems from a natural biological reaction—the body's fight-or-flight response to a perceived threat. The adrenaline rush you experience is your body preparing to deal with a challenge, but instead of needing to outrun a predator, you're preparing to navigate an interview. This adrenaline can sharpen your focus, giving you extra energy to tackle difficult questions and maintain an engaged presence. The key is learning how to channel that energy into confidence rather than fear.

One way to do this is through preparation. The more prepared you are, the less anxious you'll feel. Thoroughly researching the company, practicing your answers to common questions, and even rehearsing how you will sit, speak, and interact can reduce the unpredictability of the situation. When you know what to expect, it's easier to stay calm. Visualization is another powerful tool. Imagine yourself walking into the room confidently, shaking hands with the interviewer, and answering questions smoothly. Mentally walking through the interview before it happens helps build familiarity with

INTRODUCTION

the experience, lessening the intimidation factor.

Breathing exercises can also work wonders in calming your nerves. Slow, deep breaths can help lower your heart rate and keep you grounded. If you find yourself becoming overwhelmed, a few moments of focused breathing can help regain control over your emotions. And remember, it's okay to take a pause during the interview to collect your thoughts. Silence can feel awkward, but pausing shows you are thoughtful and methodical, traits valued by most employers.

Lastly, it's important to recognize that nerves are natural, and everyone experiences them. The interviewer likely understands this too. What sets confident candidates apart is not the absence of nerves, but the ability to manage them effectively. When you embrace your nervousness, accept it as part of the process, and transform it into focus and energy, you'll begin to notice that you don't have to get rid of anxiety to be confident. You just have to channel it in the right direction.

Who This Book is For

This book is designed for anyone who has ever walked into an interview feeling unprepared, nervous, or unsure of how to present themselves. Whether you're a first-time job seeker, a mid-career professional looking for a change, or someone who hasn't interviewed in years and is feeling out of practice, this book will provide practical strategies to boost your confidence and improve your interview performance.

If you find yourself constantly worrying about interviews, overthinking your answers, or feeling paralyzed by tough questions, this book will be particularly useful. It's for those who feel that their anxiety holds them back from presenting their best selves, and who want to transform that anxiety into a tool for success.

This book is also for individuals who are transitioning between industries, moving up in their careers, or taking on roles with new responsibilities. Interviews for leadership positions or highly specialized roles often require a deeper level of preparation and a stronger display of confidence, and this book will guide you through mastering those skills.

Additionally, this book can benefit professionals who may have the technical skills but struggle with soft skills like communication, emotional intelligence, or building rapport during interviews. Interviews are not just about what you know—they're about how you interact, how you present yourself, and how well you can communicate your value to the employer. Mastering these aspects will make you stand out, and this book will help you do just that.

Overview of the Interview Process

Before diving into strategies for mastering interviews, it's important to understand the typical process from start to finish. While each company may have its unique procedures, most interviews follow a relatively predictable path. Being familiar with the general flow of interviews can demystify the experience and make you feel more in control.

1. **Application and Pre-Screening** After submitting your resume or application, the first step often involves a pre-screening process. This might be done by a recruiter or through automated software that filters candidates based on qualifications. If your resume stands out, you'll be invited to an initial interview, which could be via phone or video.
2. **Initial Interview** The first interview is often a screening to confirm whether you meet the basic requirements of the job. This interview might be conducted by a recruiter, HR representative, or a hiring manager. During this stage, you may be asked questions about your background, experience, and why you're interested in the role. While this interview is typically shorter, it's your first chance to make a strong impression.
3. **Technical or Skill-Based Interview** Depending on the role, you may be required to participate in a technical interview or skills assessment. For technical jobs, this could involve coding challenges, portfolio reviews, or problem-solving exercises. For other positions, this might involve case studies, presentations, or task simulations. This stage tests your hard skills and how well you can apply them to real-world scenarios.
4. **Behavioral or Situational Interview** Many companies incorporate behavioral or situational interviews into their process. These types of interviews focus on how you've handled situations in the past or how

INTRODUCTION

you would handle hypothetical challenges. Questions might include "Tell me about a time when you dealt with a difficult coworker" or "How would you manage a tight deadline?" Employers use these questions to gauge your problem-solving abilities, teamwork, and leadership skills.

5. **Panel or Group Interviews** Some companies use panel interviews, where several interviewers assess you at once. This can be intimidating, but it also offers a chance to demonstrate your ability to handle pressure and engage multiple people. Group interviews, where several candidates are interviewed simultaneously, test how well you collaborate and stand out in a competitive setting.
6. **Final Interview** If you've made it this far, you're likely one of the final candidates. The final interview is usually with a higher-up or decision-maker in the company. At this stage, the focus shifts to fit—how well you align with the company culture, your long-term potential, and how you would contribute to the team. This is where your preparation and confidence really pay off.
7. **Post-Interview** After the interview, the waiting game begins. Some companies might reach out quickly, while others may take weeks to decide. During this time, sending a thoughtful thank-you email can help reinforce your interest and professionalism. If you're offered the position, salary negotiations may come into play. If you aren't selected, it's a great opportunity to ask for feedback and continue improving for future interviews.

Understanding this process not only prepares you mentally but also allows you to anticipate what's coming, thereby reducing anxiety. As you read through this book, you'll gain the skills to confidently navigate each stage of the interview process, from the initial screening to the final handshake, transforming your nerves into a source of strength along the way.

Chapter 1: Understanding the Interview Mindset

Your mindset going into an interview is just as important as the knowledge and experience you bring to the table. Often, what distinguishes successful candidates from those who struggle isn't their skillset or qualifications but the way they approach the interview mentally. Interviews are unique high-stress situations that require not only technical proficiency but also the right psychological approach. This chapter will guide you through understanding and mastering the interview mindset by addressing the psychology of fear, reframing the interview as a conversation, building a growth mindset, and highlighting the key differences between a nervous and confident candidate.

The Psychology of Fear and How to Overcome It

One of the biggest hurdles people face in interviews is fear. Fear of failure, fear of rejection, fear of not being good enough—these emotions can sabotage an otherwise well-prepared candidate. It's crucial to understand where this fear comes from and how to deal with it in a productive manner.

Fear is a natural response rooted in our evolutionary history. In high-pressure situations, our brain perceives the interview as a threat, triggering a fight-or-flight response. The adrenaline rush that follows is meant to prepare the body to either fight or flee. While this reaction was useful when facing physical threats, it's less helpful in modern scenarios like interviews, where calmness, poise, and clear thinking are essential.

Understanding that fear is a natural biological response is the first step in

CHAPTER 1: UNDERSTANDING THE INTERVIEW MINDSET

overcoming it. Recognizing that your body is simply reacting to a perceived threat, not an actual one, helps demystify the anxiety you're experiencing. When you feel your heart racing or notice that you're sweating, instead of interpreting those signs as weaknesses, realize that your body is trying to help you perform at a heightened level. The key is to channel that heightened energy productively rather than letting it paralyze you.

One practical way to deal with interview fear is by breaking down the scenario. Most of the fear comes from the unknown—the "what ifs." What if I stumble on my words? What if they ask something I don't know? What if I get rejected? To mitigate these concerns, preparation becomes your strongest ally. The more familiar you are with the questions, the format, and even the people you'll be speaking with, the less fear will take hold. Researching the company and practicing your responses to common questions makes the interview feel less like a high-stakes test and more like a task you're equipped to handle.

Another critical tool in overcoming fear is reframing your mindset around failure. Many people approach interviews with the idea that failure is catastrophic. But what if, instead, you viewed failure as a learning opportunity? Every interview, even one that doesn't go as planned, is an experience you can draw from for future opportunities. Shifting your focus from perfection to growth reduces the fear of failure, making it easier to navigate tough questions or moments where you feel you've stumbled.

Additionally, learning breathing techniques can help regulate your nervous system. Deep, controlled breaths send signals to your brain that it's okay to relax. This simple but effective method can be employed at any stage during the interview—from right before you walk in, to during difficult questions, and even in between interviews as a way to reset.

Visualization is another powerful technique for reducing interview fear. Instead of focusing on potential negative outcomes, visualize yourself succeeding. Imagine walking into the room with confidence, answering questions clearly, and leaving the interview feeling satisfied with your performance. This mental rehearsal primes your brain to expect success, making it more likely that you'll perform well.

Finally, remember that fear is not inherently bad. Even the most seasoned professionals experience nerves before an important interview. The key is to not let that fear control you. Instead, use it as a reminder that you care about the outcome. When you face fear head-on, acknowledge it, and implement strategies to manage it, you'll find that it no longer holds the power it once did.

Reframing Interviews as Conversations

One of the most effective ways to overcome interview anxiety and build confidence is by reframing the interview itself. Many candidates view interviews as tests where they are being judged on their worthiness. This mindset puts the interviewer in a position of power, while the candidate is left feeling vulnerable and exposed. However, interviews are not one-sided interrogations. When you reframe the interview as a conversation rather than a test, you can approach it with less pressure and more curiosity.

Think of interviews as collaborative discussions between two parties that are trying to figure out whether they are a good match. The interviewer is not just assessing you; they are also trying to sell the company and the role. If they've brought you in for an interview, it means they already see potential in you. Your job now is to engage with them in a meaningful dialogue to determine whether this role fits your career goals and values.

Viewing the interview as a conversation helps shift the dynamic from one of fear to one of mutual exploration. Instead of thinking, "Will they like me?" shift your focus to, "Is this the right opportunity for me?" This change in mindset not only reduces anxiety but also allows you to bring your true self to the interview.

A conversational approach also encourages active listening. Interviews aren't just about your answers; they're about how well you engage with the interviewer. When you listen attentively to their questions, you can offer more thoughtful responses. Likewise, asking insightful questions shows that you're invested in the role and the company. Questions like "Can you describe the team dynamics?" or "What are some challenges the company is currently facing?" turn the interview into a two-way conversation and demonstrate that you're thinking about your fit within the organization.

CHAPTER 1: UNDERSTANDING THE INTERVIEW MINDSET

Conversations are inherently more relaxed than tests. They allow for more flexibility and give you the opportunity to recover from mistakes. If you stumble on an answer, you can course-correct as the conversation unfolds. Unlike a written test, where every wrong answer is final, interviews provide opportunities for clarification and deeper engagement. This flexibility should ease some of the pressure.

Another benefit of reframing the interview as a conversation is that it helps you build rapport with the interviewer. People are more likely to hire individuals they like and feel comfortable with. By engaging the interviewer in a dialogue, sharing stories, and finding common ground, you humanize the interaction. When an interviewer feels a connection with you, they're more likely to view your qualifications in a positive light.

Reframing the interview also shifts your body language and tone. When you're nervous, your posture may be rigid, your tone flat, and your gestures minimal. However, when you're engaged in a conversation, you naturally relax. Your body language opens up, your tone becomes more animated, and your facial expressions reflect your engagement. These non-verbal cues significantly impact how the interviewer perceives you.

In essence, the interview is an exchange of value. You bring your skills, experience, and enthusiasm, while the company offers an opportunity for growth, learning, and advancement. Both parties are assessing whether this exchange benefits them. Approaching the interview with this mindset takes it out of the realm of judgment and turns it into a collaborative dialogue where both you and the employer have equal roles.

Building a Growth Mindset: Embrace Learning

Adopting a growth mindset can revolutionize your approach to interviews. A growth mindset, a concept popularized by psychologist Carol Dweck, is the belief that abilities and intelligence can be developed over time through effort, learning, and perseverance. In contrast, a fixed mindset assumes that your abilities are static and unchangeable. Those with a fixed mindset tend to view challenges as threats to their competence, while those with a growth mindset see challenges as opportunities to learn and grow.

In the context of interviews, candidates with a fixed mindset might see the process as a pass/fail test of their worth. They fear making mistakes because they believe mistakes reveal a lack of ability. On the other hand, candidates with a growth mindset view interviews as a learning experience. Every question, every challenge, and even every mistake becomes an opportunity to improve.

When you approach an interview with a growth mindset, you don't feel the need to be perfect. Instead, you focus on learning from each experience. If you don't know the answer to a question, you don't panic or feel like a failure. Instead, you acknowledge that this is an area where you can grow. This openness to learning makes you more adaptable and resilient, qualities that interviewers appreciate.

One way to cultivate a growth mindset is by reflecting on past interview experiences. Instead of focusing solely on the outcome (whether you got the job or not), think about what you learned from the process. Did you discover a gap in your knowledge? Did you identify areas where you can improve your communication skills? By analyzing your performance with the goal of growth, you can continuously improve, making each interview better than the last.

A growth mindset also helps you remain curious and open during the interview itself. Instead of worrying about giving the "right" answer, you can approach questions with curiosity and an eagerness to engage in dialogue. For example, if an interviewer asks a difficult or unexpected question, instead of seeing it as a potential pitfall, view it as an opportunity to showcase your problem-solving skills. Even if you don't have the perfect answer, your ability to think on your feet and demonstrate a willingness to learn can leave a positive impression.

Another important aspect of the growth mindset is resilience. Interviews don't always go as planned. You might stumble, make mistakes, or face tough competition. But with a growth mindset, setbacks aren't the end of the road—they're stepping stones to future success. Rejection from one role doesn't define your potential. It simply provides feedback that can help you improve for the next opportunity. This resilience is what allows confident candidates to bounce back from failures and continue pursuing their career goals.

CHAPTER 1: UNDERSTANDING THE INTERVIEW MINDSET

Embracing a growth mindset also means being open to feedback. Many candidates shy away from seeking feedback after an unsuccessful interview because it can be uncomfortable to hear where they fell short. However, constructive criticism is one of the most valuable tools for improvement. By welcoming feedback and actively seeking it out, you demonstrate a commitment to growth and learning, which are attractive qualities to employers.

In summary, developing a growth mindset transforms the way you approach interviews. Rather than fearing failure, you view challenges as opportunities to learn. By reflecting on past experiences, remaining curious, building resilience, and welcoming feedback, you equip yourself with the tools necessary to navigate any interview situation with confidence and poise.

Key Differences Between a Nervous and Confident Candidate

Understanding the distinction between nervous and confident candidates can illuminate how to develop your interview mindset. Nervous candidates often present themselves in ways that undermine their qualifications, while confident candidates exude a sense of assurance and self-worth. Recognizing these differences can provide valuable insights into how to portray yourself more effectively during interviews.

1. **Body Language** Nervous candidates typically display closed-off body language. They may fidget, avoid eye contact, or have a rigid posture, all of which can signal insecurity and a lack of confidence. In contrast, confident candidates adopt open and relaxed body language. They maintain eye contact, smile genuinely, and use gestures that indicate engagement. A confident posture—standing or sitting up straight, with shoulders back—communicates assurance and readiness.
2. **Communication Style** Nervous candidates may speak in a hesitant or soft voice, often mumbling or rushing through their answers. This can

make it difficult for the interviewer to engage with them fully. Confident candidates, on the other hand, speak clearly and at a steady pace. They articulate their thoughts well, using pauses effectively to emphasize important points. Their tone is steady and assured, making them more persuasive and engaging.

3. **Preparation** While both nervous and confident candidates may prepare for their interviews, the depth of their preparation differs. Nervous candidates may focus solely on rehearsing answers to common questions, often fixating on "perfect" responses. This can create additional pressure to perform flawlessly. Confident candidates, however, prepare holistically. They not only practice answers but also research the company and industry, anticipate potential questions, and think critically about their personal fit within the organization. Their broader preparation equips them to adapt and pivot during the interview, making them more resilient to unexpected questions.

4. **Handling Difficult Questions** Nervous candidates often struggle with challenging questions. They may freeze, stumble over their words, or provide inadequate answers, which can negatively impact the interview. Confident candidates, however, view difficult questions as opportunities to demonstrate their critical thinking and problem-solving skills. When faced with a tough question, they take a moment to gather their thoughts, respond thoughtfully, and may even ask clarifying questions to ensure they understand the interviewer's intent. This calm and collected demeanor speaks volumes about their confidence.

5. **Asking Questions** Nervous candidates might avoid asking questions during the interview, fearing that they'll appear uninformed or unprepared. This lack of engagement can hinder rapport-building and leave interviewers with a negative impression. Confident candidates actively engage by asking insightful questions about the company, role, or team dynamics. Their inquiries reflect their interest and enthusiasm while also providing them with valuable information to assess their own fit for the position.

6. **Posture and Presence** The presence a candidate brings into the

CHAPTER 1: UNDERSTANDING THE INTERVIEW MINDSET

interview room plays a crucial role in how they are perceived. Nervous candidates may enter the room with their heads down, appearing timid and uncertain. In contrast, confident candidates walk in with a sense of purpose. They greet interviewers warmly, introducing themselves with a firm handshake and a friendly smile. Their strong presence creates an immediate sense of trust and respect.

7. **Mindset on Feedback** Nervous candidates often take feedback personally, viewing it as a judgment of their worth or abilities. This mindset can be damaging and prevent them from learning and growing from experiences. Confident candidates, however, welcome feedback as an essential part of their growth journey. They understand that feedback is not a reflection of their value but rather a means of improving their skills and performance.

8. **Outcome Focus** Nervous candidates often obsess over the outcome of the interview, worrying about whether they'll be hired or rejected. This focus can lead to anxiety and hinder their performance. Confident candidates concentrate on the process, engaging fully in the conversation and showcasing their capabilities. They recognize that interviews are a two-way street and focus on finding the right fit for themselves as well.

In summary, understanding the differences between nervous and confident candidates is essential for developing the right interview mindset. By adopting confident body language, effective communication styles, and an open mindset toward feedback and learning, you can present yourself more favorably in interviews. Ultimately, confidence is not just about projecting assurance; it's about believing in your ability to succeed and learning from every experience along the way.

Chapter 2: Preparation is Key: Researching the Company and Role

Preparation is the backbone of a successful job interview. It goes beyond rehearsing answers to common questions; it involves thoroughly researching the company and understanding the role you are applying for. This chapter will delve into why research is essential, how to leverage various resources effectively, how to analyze the job description, match your skills to the employer's needs, and create a cheat sheet to guide you during the interview. By the end of this chapter, you will be equipped with the knowledge and tools necessary to present yourself as a well-informed and confident candidate.

Why Research Matters

Researching the company and the role is crucial for several reasons. It not only equips you with relevant information to answer questions confidently but also demonstrates your genuine interest in the position and the organization.

1. **Shows Your Commitment** Conducting thorough research indicates to interviewers that you are serious about the job and willing to invest time and effort into understanding the organization. This commitment can set you apart from other candidates who may have come unprepared.
2. **Enables Tailored Responses** When you understand the company's culture, values, and current initiatives, you can tailor your responses to

resonate with the interviewers. This makes your answers more relevant and engaging, helping you connect with the panel.
3. **Helps You Ask Insightful Questions** Research enables you to formulate thoughtful questions that go beyond the basics. Asking questions related to recent company developments, future projects, or challenges faced by the organization demonstrates your proactive attitude and enthusiasm for the role.
4. **Informs Your Self-Presentation** Knowing the company's goals and the role's expectations allows you to align your strengths and experiences with what the employer is looking for. You can emphasize specific achievements and skills that are most relevant, making your case more compelling.
5. **Mitigates Anxiety** When you are well-prepared, you will feel more confident going into the interview. Knowledge reduces uncertainty and anxiety, allowing you to focus on showcasing your qualifications and personality.
6. **Gives You Context for Situational Questions** Many interviewers may pose situational questions that pertain directly to the company's operations or challenges. By being informed about the organization, you can provide relevant examples and solutions that demonstrate your problem-solving abilities.

Overall, thorough research allows you to approach the interview with confidence, articulate your value effectively, and establish a rapport with the interviewers.

Using Company Websites, Glassdoor, and LinkedIn Effectively

The internet is a treasure trove of information that can help you prepare for interviews. Here's how to utilize key platforms effectively:

1. Company Websites

- **About Us Page**: Start with the company's official website, particularly the "About Us" page. This section typically includes the company's mission, vision, values, and history. Understanding these elements can help you frame your responses and demonstrate alignment with the organization's culture.
- **Products and Services**: Familiarize yourself with the company's products, services, and recent innovations. This knowledge will allow you to discuss how your skills can contribute to their offerings.
- **News and Events**: Look for a section on news or press releases to stay updated on recent developments, awards, or community involvement. Being informed about recent news can help you ask insightful questions during the interview.
- **Career Page**: Explore the career section to understand what qualities the company values in its employees. You can also find information about employee benefits, work culture, and professional development opportunities.
- **Company Blog**: If available, read through the company blog to gain insights into the organization's voice, expertise, and industry trends.

2. Glassdoor

- **Company Reviews**: Glassdoor provides employee reviews that can offer valuable insights into the work culture, management styles, and the overall employee experience. While reviews can be subjective, they can give you a glimpse into the company's strengths and weaknesses.
- **Salary Information**: Use Glassdoor to research salary ranges for the role you're applying for. This information will help you understand the market rate and prepare you for potential salary discussions.
- **Interview Experiences**: Glassdoor also features interview experiences shared by past candidates. Reading through these experiences can help you anticipate the types of questions you may face and understand the

interview process.

3. LinkedIn

- **Company Profile**: Visit the company's LinkedIn page to find additional information about their operations, recent updates, and connections within the industry. LinkedIn is also a great resource for understanding the company's mission and values through shared posts and articles.
- **Employee Connections**: If you know anyone working at the company, reach out for informational interviews. Current employees can provide insider knowledge about the culture and hiring process.
- **Industry Trends**: Use LinkedIn to follow industry leaders and influencers. Engaging with relevant content can keep you informed about trends and challenges in the industry, which can be helpful during your interview.

4. Social Media

- **Company Social Media Accounts**: Follow the company on platforms like Twitter, Facebook, and Instagram. This can give you a sense of the company's culture, values, and how they engage with their customers and community.
- **Employee Engagement**: Pay attention to how employees interact on social media. Employee posts and engagement can provide insight into the company culture and workplace environment.

By leveraging these resources, you will gather a wealth of information that can enhance your understanding of the company and role, ultimately preparing you for a successful interview.

Understanding the Job Description

The job description is a critical document that outlines the responsibilities, qualifications, and expectations of the role you are applying for. Understanding this document is key to effective preparation.

1. **Breaking Down the Job Description** Start by carefully reviewing the job description. Break it down into key components, including responsibilities, required skills, qualifications, and preferred attributes.

   - **Responsibilities**: Note the primary tasks associated with the role. Identify which responsibilities you have experience with and be prepared to discuss relevant examples during the interview.
   - **Required Skills**: Highlight the essential skills the employer seeks. These can range from technical abilities to soft skills. Make a list of your own skills that match those outlined in the description.
   - **Qualifications**: Pay attention to the required education and experience levels. If you meet or exceed these qualifications, be prepared to discuss your background in relation to them.
   - **Preferred Attributes**: Often, job descriptions will include preferred qualifications or attributes. While these may not be essential, mentioning any relevant experiences or qualities can strengthen your candidacy.

1. **Identifying Keywords** Look for keywords and phrases that are frequently repeated in the job description. These terms can provide insight into the company's priorities and the specific traits they value in candidates. Incorporate these keywords into your answers and resume to align your application with the job requirements.
2. **Aligning Your Experiences** Reflect on your past experiences and identify examples that align with the responsibilities and qualifications listed in the job description. Use the STAR method (Situation, Task, Action, Result) to frame your responses effectively during the interview.
3. **Researching Trends in the Industry** Understanding the broader

CHAPTER 2: PREPARATION IS KEY: RESEARCHING THE COMPANY AND...

context of the role within the industry can enhance your answers. Research current trends, challenges, and opportunities relevant to the position. This knowledge will enable you to discuss how you can contribute to the company's success.

4. **Anticipating Questions** As you analyze the job description, consider potential questions the interviewer might ask based on the listed responsibilities and qualifications. Prepare answers that address these anticipated questions.
5. **Understanding the Company's Goals** Align your understanding of the job description with the company's overall mission and goals. Discuss how your role contributes to the organization's success and aligns with its values. This alignment can strengthen your position as a candidate.

By fully understanding the job description and aligning your experiences with the employer's expectations, you will be better prepared to showcase your qualifications during the interview.

Matching Your Skills with What the Company Wants

Once you have a clear understanding of the job description, the next step is to match your skills and experiences with what the company wants. This alignment is crucial for effectively demonstrating your fit for the role.

1. **Conduct a Skills Inventory** Take stock of your skills, qualifications, and experiences. Create a list of your technical skills, soft skills, and relevant experiences that pertain to the job you're applying for. This inventory will serve as a reference during your interview preparation.

   - **Technical Skills**: List skills related to the specific technical requirements of the job, such as programming languages, software proficiency, or industry-specific knowledge.
   - **Soft Skills**: Identify essential soft skills, such as communication, teamwork, adaptability, and problem-solving. Consider how these skills have

been demonstrated in your past experiences.

1. **Create a Skills Matrix** A skills matrix can help visualize how your experiences align with the job requirements. Create a table with two columns: one for the skills listed in the job description and one for your corresponding experiences or achievements. This exercise will clarify your strengths and areas of alignment.
2. Job RequirementsYour Relevant Experiences
3. Project Management
4. Led a team to complete a project ahead of schedule, coordinating resources and timelines.
5. Data Analysis
6. Analyzed sales data to identify trends and recommend strategies, leading to a 15% increase in revenue.
7. Strong Communication
8. Presented quarterly updates to stakeholders, ensuring alignment and transparency in project progress.
9. **Craft Compelling Stories** Prepare stories that highlight your relevant experiences and accomplishments. Use the STAR method to structure these stories, ensuring they are concise and impactful. Focus on quantifiable results to demonstrate the value you brought to previous roles.
10. **Identify Unique Selling Points** Consider what sets you apart from other candidates. Identify unique experiences, skills, or perspectives that can add value to the organization. This can be a particular achievement, a relevant certification, or a unique perspective based on your background.
11. **Practice Articulating Your Skills** Practice articulating how your skills align with the role. Use mock interviews to refine your delivery and ensure you can effectively communicate your qualifications. Pay attention to how you frame your experiences in relation to the job requirements.
12. **Demonstrate Enthusiasm for Learning** Employers appreciate candidates who are willing to learn and grow. If there are skills or

experiences you lack but are relevant to the role, express your eagerness to develop those areas. Share examples of how you have pursued learning opportunities in the past.

By aligning your skills with what the company wants, you will present yourself as a strong candidate who is not only qualified but also genuinely interested in contributing to the organization's success.

Creating Your Cheat Sheet: Key Facts and Talking Points

Creating a cheat sheet is an effective way to consolidate your research and prepare for the interview. This document serves as a quick reference guide, allowing you to recall key facts and talking points during the interview.

1. **Key Company Facts** Compile essential information about the company, including its mission, values, history, and recent developments. Highlight any awards, recognition, or community initiatives that resonate with you. This information can serve as conversation starters or points of reference during the interview.

- **Example**: "I was impressed to learn that your company was recognized as one of the top employers in the region for promoting employee wellness. This aligns with my values of fostering a healthy work-life balance."

1. **Role-Specific Information** Summarize the job description, highlighting key responsibilities and qualifications. Include your matching skills and experiences for each requirement to facilitate quick recall during the interview.
2. **Questions to Ask** Prepare a list of insightful questions to ask the interviewer. These questions can revolve around company culture, team dynamics, and future projects. Thoughtful questions demonstrate your interest in the role and the organization.

- **Example**: "I noticed that your company recently launched a new sustainability initiative. Can you share more about how this impacts your team's goals and projects?"

1. **Personal Achievements and Stories** Include a brief summary of your key achievements and stories that highlight your relevant experiences. Use bullet points for quick reference, ensuring you can easily recall these examples during the conversation.

- **Example Achievement**: "In my last role, I increased sales by 25% through targeted marketing campaigns. This involved analyzing customer data and adjusting our strategy accordingly."

1. **Visual Presentation** Create your cheat sheet in a visually appealing format. Use bullet points, headings, and bold text to make it easy to skim. Keep it concise, aiming for one to two pages, so it is manageable and does not overwhelm you.
2. **Practice with Your Cheat Sheet** Use your cheat sheet as a reference during mock interviews or practice sessions. Familiarize yourself with the content so that it becomes a natural extension of your preparation. This will help you feel more confident when discussing key points during the actual interview.
3. **Review and Update** Continually review and update your cheat sheet as you gather more information or as the interview date approaches. Tailoring the content to specific interviews can enhance your preparation and make your responses more relevant.

Thorough preparation is essential for success in any job interview. By understanding why research matters, effectively utilizing various resources, analyzing the job description, matching your skills to the company's needs, and creating a cheat sheet, you will be well-equipped to present yourself as a confident and knowledgeable candidate. This preparation not only enhances your performance during the interview but also demonstrates your genuine interest in the role and the organization, setting the stage for a successful conversation. With these tools and strategies in hand, you will be ready to ace every interview you face.

Chapter 3: Mastering Your Personal Pitch

In the competitive world of job interviews, your personal pitch is one of the most critical elements in creating a positive first impression. It sets the tone for the entire conversation and can greatly influence how interviewers perceive your qualifications and fit for the role. This chapter will delve into mastering your personal pitch, focusing on crafting a compelling elevator pitch, perfecting the often-asked "Tell me about yourself" question, and sharing your unique story that highlights your achievements, values, and passions. Additionally, we will explore how to adapt your pitch to various interview formats to ensure that you resonate with different audiences.

How to Create an Elevator Pitch

An elevator pitch is a brief, persuasive speech that you can use to spark interest in what you do or in a particular project or idea. It should be concise enough to deliver in the time it takes to ride an elevator—typically 30 to 60 seconds. Crafting an effective elevator pitch is essential because it allows you to present your skills and aspirations clearly and confidently, laying the groundwork for a successful interview.

1. **Define Your Objective** The first step in creating an elevator pitch is to clarify your objective. What do you want the listener to know about you? Are you highlighting your qualifications for a specific role, your skills, or your passion for the industry? Your pitch should be tailored to the context, so identifying the main goal will guide the content you include.
2. **Structure Your Pitch** A well-structured elevator pitch typically con-

tains three key components:

- **Who You Are**: Start with a brief introduction that includes your name and current position or professional background. This sets the context for the listener.
- **What You Do**: Clearly articulate what you do. This should include your skills, experience, and what makes you unique. Focus on your value proposition—what you bring to the table.
- **What You Want**: End your pitch by stating your objective. This could be a desire to connect, learn more about a specific opportunity, or a call to action, such as scheduling a follow-up meeting.

1. **Use Engaging Language** To capture your listener's attention, use engaging and vivid language. Avoid jargon or overly technical terms that may confuse the audience. Instead, use relatable language that reflects your personality. The goal is to sound natural, authentic, and enthusiastic about what you do.
2. **Be Authentic** Authenticity is critical in any personal pitch. Your audience will connect more with you if they sense that you are genuine. Share a brief anecdote or personal story that relates to your skills or career journey. This not only makes your pitch more engaging but also helps you stand out in a sea of candidates.
3. **Practice, Practice, Practice** Once you've crafted your elevator pitch, practice delivering it. Focus on your tone, pace, and body language. It's important to sound confident but not rehearsed. Practicing in front of a mirror or recording yourself can help you refine your delivery and identify areas for improvement.
4. **Seek Feedback** Getting feedback from trusted colleagues, friends, or mentors can provide valuable insights. They can offer suggestions on what resonates well and what might need adjustment. Constructive criticism can help you refine your pitch further.
5. **Be Flexible** Your elevator pitch should be adaptable depending on the context. For example, if you're networking at an event, you might want

to focus more on your current projects, whereas in a formal interview, you might emphasize your skills relevant to the job. Being flexible ensures that you connect effectively with your audience.

By following these steps, you can create an engaging elevator pitch that captures your unique professional identity and opens the door to meaningful conversations. An effective elevator pitch is an essential tool in your job search arsenal, empowering you to present yourself confidently in interviews, networking events, and professional interactions.

Perfecting the "Tell Me About Yourself" Answer

The "Tell me about yourself" question is one of the most common—and often dreaded—interview prompts. This question is a chance for you to introduce yourself to the interviewer, so it's vital to craft a response that highlights your qualifications while also showcasing your personality.

1. **Start with a Strong Opening** Your opening should grab the interviewer's attention and set the stage for the rest of your response. You might begin with a brief statement about your professional background, such as, "I'm a marketing professional with over five years of experience in digital marketing and brand strategy." This clear statement helps the interviewer understand your expertise from the outset.
2. **Follow the "Present-Past-Future" Structure** A commonly recommended approach to answering this question is the "Present-Past-Future" structure, which helps you present a coherent narrative about your career journey.

- **Present**: Start by discussing your current role, including your responsibilities, achievements, and what you enjoy about your work. This establishes your current qualifications.
- **Past**: Next, briefly describe your past experiences that led you to your current position. Highlight relevant skills or accomplishments that demonstrate your growth and development.
- **Future**: Finally, discuss your future aspirations. Explain why you are

excited about this particular opportunity and how it aligns with your career goals. This not only shows your enthusiasm for the position but also your forward-thinking mindset.

1. **Highlight Key Achievements** While discussing your experiences, make sure to include specific achievements that showcase your skills and expertise. Quantifying your accomplishments can make them more impactful. For example, you might say, "In my current role, I led a project that increased our social media engagement by 40% within three months." Concrete numbers provide evidence of your capabilities.

2. **Showcase Your Values and Personality** Your answer should reflect your personality and values. Consider incorporating elements that highlight what you are passionate about and what drives you professionally. For instance, you might say, "I'm particularly passionate about using data to drive marketing decisions because I believe that understanding our audience leads to more meaningful connections."

3. **Keep it Concise** While it's essential to provide enough detail to be engaging, aim to keep your response concise—around two to three minutes is usually ideal. The goal is to provide a snapshot of your professional journey without overwhelming the interviewer with too much information.

4. **Practice Delivery** Once you've crafted your response, practice delivering it. Focus on maintaining a conversational tone and ensuring that your body language is open and inviting. Practicing in front of a friend or recording yourself can help you refine your delivery and ensure that you sound confident and engaging.

5. **Be Prepared for Follow-Up Questions** Your answer to this question may lead to follow-up questions, so be prepared to elaborate on specific points or provide more details about your experiences. This is an opportunity to demonstrate your expertise and further engage the interviewer in conversation.

6. **Tailor Your Answer to the Role** While your answer should provide an overview of your career, it's essential to tailor it to the specific role for

which you are interviewing. Highlight experiences and skills that are particularly relevant to the position, and convey your genuine interest in the company and its mission.

By perfecting your response to the "Tell me about yourself" question, you can set a positive tone for the rest of the interview. This prompt is not just a chance to talk about your qualifications; it's an opportunity to showcase your personality and values, allowing the interviewer to connect with you on a more personal level.

Crafting Your Story: Achievements, Values, and Passion

Your personal story is a powerful tool in the interview process. It allows you to connect with interviewers on a deeper level, showcasing not only your qualifications but also your achievements, values, and passions. Crafting a compelling story is essential for creating a memorable impression and standing out from other candidates.

1. **Identify Key Themes in Your Story** To begin crafting your story, identify key themes that resonate with your professional journey. Consider significant moments, achievements, or challenges that have shaped your career. These themes will provide a narrative framework that ties together your experiences and showcases your growth.
2. **Showcase Achievements with Impact** When discussing your achievements, focus on the impact they had on your team or organization. Instead of merely listing your accomplishments, explain how your contributions made a difference. For example, rather than saying, "I completed a project on time," you might say, "I led a project that not only met the deadline but also resulted in a 25% increase in customer satisfaction." This approach highlights your ability to deliver results.
3. **Connect Your Values to Your Work** Your values play a crucial role in shaping your career path and decisions. When crafting your story, consider how your values align with your professional experiences. For instance, if collaboration and teamwork are important to you, share examples of how you've worked effectively with others to achieve

common goals. Connecting your values to your work demonstrates authenticity and allows interviewers to see the person behind the qualifications.

4. **Highlight Your Passion** Passion is contagious. When you talk about what excites you, it draws others in and creates a positive impression. Share what you are passionate about within your field, whether it's a specific project, a particular aspect of your work, or a broader mission. For example, you might say, "I'm passionate about developing innovative marketing strategies that connect brands with their audiences. I believe that storytelling is a powerful tool for building authentic relationships."

5. **Craft a Narrative Arc** Structure your story with a clear beginning, middle, and end. Start with an engaging introduction that captures attention, then delve into the challenges you faced, the actions you took, and the results you achieved. This narrative arc helps create a compelling flow, making it easier for interviewers to follow along and remember your story.

6. **Use Vivid Language and Details** To make your story memorable, use vivid language and specific details that evoke imagery. Instead of saying, "I improved team communication," you might say, "I initiated weekly check-in meetings that fostered open dialogue among team members, resulting in a more collaborative and efficient work environment." These details create a more engaging picture for the listener.

7. **Practice Telling Your Story** Practice delivering your story until it feels natural. Aim for a conversational tone, and don't be afraid to inject your personality into your storytelling. Practicing in front of a mirror or with a friend can help you refine your delivery and ensure that your passion comes through.

8. **Be Open to Adaptation** Your story should be adaptable depending on the context. While you may have a core narrative, be prepared to adjust the details based on the specific role or interview format. This adaptability shows that you can think on your feet and tailor your approach to the audience.

By crafting a compelling personal story that highlights your achievements, values, and passions, you create a powerful narrative that resonates with interviewers. Your story not only conveys your qualifications but also establishes a connection that can leave a lasting impression.

Adapting Your Pitch to Different Interview Formats

Different interview formats require different approaches to your personal pitch. Whether you're participating in a one-on-one interview, a panel interview, or a virtual interview, adapting your pitch ensures that you connect effectively with your audience.

1. **One-on-One Interviews** In a traditional one-on-one interview, your pitch should focus on establishing rapport with the interviewer. Start with a warm greeting, and deliver your elevator pitch or "Tell me about yourself" response confidently. Pay attention to the interviewer's reactions and adjust your delivery based on their cues. Use their body language and feedback to gauge their interest and engagement.

2. **Panel Interviews** Panel interviews involve multiple interviewers, and your pitch should address the entire panel. Make eye contact with each panelist as you introduce yourself and present your pitch. This inclusivity helps establish connections with all members of the panel. Tailor your responses to the different interviewers, addressing their areas of expertise or focus as appropriate. This shows that you are attentive and respectful of their roles in the interview process.

3. **Group Interviews** In group interviews, where multiple candidates are interviewed simultaneously, it's essential to differentiate yourself. While delivering your pitch, maintain a positive and engaging demeanor. Avoid being overly competitive or dismissive of others; instead, focus on showcasing your unique strengths. Acknowledge your fellow candidates and encourage collaboration. This demonstrates teamwork and adaptability, which are valued traits in many roles.

4. **Virtual Interviews** With the rise of remote work, virtual interviews have become increasingly common. When delivering your pitch in a virtual format, pay attention to your background, lighting, and camera

positioning. Ensure that you are dressed appropriately and that your technology is functioning properly. During your pitch, maintain eye contact by looking directly at the camera rather than the screen. This creates a more personal connection, even in a virtual setting.

5. **Networking Events and Informal Interviews** Networking events often provide opportunities for informal conversations with potential employers. Your pitch should be even more concise in these settings. Be prepared to introduce yourself quickly and make a positive impression in just a minute or two. Focus on creating a connection rather than delivering a rehearsed pitch. Use open-ended questions to engage the other person in conversation and express genuine interest in their work.

6. **Tailoring Your Content** Regardless of the interview format, always tailor your content to the specific role and organization. Research the company's values, culture, and recent developments. This knowledge will help you align your pitch with the organization's goals and demonstrate your enthusiasm for contributing to their success.

7. **Being Mindful of Time** In interviews, time is often limited. Be mindful of how long your pitch takes, ensuring that you leave room for questions and discussions. A well-timed pitch not only showcases your ability to communicate effectively but also indicates your respect for the interviewer's time.

8. **Practicing Adaptability** Finally, practice adapting your pitch to different formats. Role-play with a friend or mentor, simulating various interview scenarios. This practice will help you become comfortable adjusting your delivery based on the audience and setting.

By mastering the art of adapting your personal pitch to different interview formats, you enhance your ability to connect with interviewers and leave a lasting impression. Each format presents unique opportunities and challenges, and being prepared to navigate them will contribute to your overall success in the interview process.

BRAVE AND PREPARED: ELEVATE YOUR INTERVIEW GAME

Mastering your personal pitch is a crucial aspect of the interview process that can significantly impact your success. By creating a compelling elevator pitch, perfecting your response to the "Tell me about yourself" question, crafting your story, and adapting your pitch to various interview formats, you equip yourself with the tools to present yourself confidently and authentically. The ability to articulate your value, achievements, and passions effectively can set you apart from other candidates and create a lasting impression on interviewers. As you continue to refine your personal pitch, remember that practice, authenticity, and adaptability are key to acing every interview you face.

Chapter 4: Anticipating Common Interview Questions

Interviews can be intimidating, especially when it comes to the uncertainty of the questions you may face. However, being prepared can transform that anxiety into confidence. This chapter will help you anticipate common interview questions, providing strategies for effectively addressing both behavioral and technical questions, mastering the STAR method for structured answers, and handling unexpected or curveball inquiries. By the end, you will be equipped to approach interviews with greater ease and assurance.

Behavioral vs. Technical Questions: How to Approach Them

Understanding the distinction between behavioral and technical questions is vital for effective preparation. Both types of questions serve different purposes and require different strategies.

1. **Behavioral Questions** Behavioral questions focus on your past experiences and how they relate to the skills needed for the job. These questions are based on the premise that past behavior is the best predictor of future performance. Interviewers use them to assess how you have handled specific situations and challenges in your previous roles.

- **Examples of Behavioral Questions**:
- "Can you describe a time when you had to deal with a difficult coworker?"

- "Tell me about a project you led and the outcome."
- "How do you prioritize your work when you have multiple deadlines?"
- **Approach**: To answer behavioral questions effectively, use the STAR method (Situation, Task, Action, Result), which we will discuss in more detail later in this chapter. Prepare several anecdotes from your work experience that illustrate your skills, adaptability, and problem-solving abilities.

1. **Technical Questions** Technical questions assess your knowledge and expertise in a particular field or skill set. These questions may involve problem-solving, practical applications, or theoretical knowledge specific to the role you're applying for.

   - **Examples of Technical Questions**:
   - "What is the difference between a primary key and a foreign key in a database?"
   - "Can you explain how you would troubleshoot a network issue?"
   - "Describe the process you would use to analyze a data set."
   - **Approach**: To effectively handle technical questions, first, ensure you have a strong understanding of the core concepts and skills relevant to your field. Review job descriptions and industry trends to identify key areas of focus. Practice answering potential technical questions, either through mock interviews or study groups, to enhance your confidence.

1. **Combining Both Types** In many interviews, you will encounter a mix of behavioral and technical questions. Recognize the context of each question and adjust your response accordingly. For example, if asked about a technical challenge you faced, provide a behavioral response that illustrates your approach and problem-solving skills, along with any relevant technical details.
2. **Tailoring Your Responses** Regardless of the question type, tailor your responses to align with the values and expectations of the organization. Research the company culture and job requirements to ensure that your

CHAPTER 4: ANTICIPATING COMMON INTERVIEW QUESTIONS

answers highlight qualities that the employer is seeking. For example, if a company emphasizes collaboration, share examples that demonstrate your ability to work effectively within a team.
3. **Staying Calm and Composed** When faced with challenging questions, it's essential to remain calm and composed. Take a moment to think about your response before answering, especially for technical questions. If you're unsure about a technical concept, it's okay to admit it, but express a willingness to learn or discuss related topics you are knowledgeable about.

By understanding the differences between behavioral and technical questions and preparing accordingly, you will approach interviews with confidence and clarity.

The STAR Method: Structuring Your Answers

The STAR method is an effective technique for answering behavioral questions in interviews. It provides a structured way to convey your experiences and accomplishments, ensuring that your responses are clear, concise, and impactful.

1. **Situation** Start by describing the context of your experience. Set the stage for the interviewer by providing relevant background information. Explain the situation, including where and when it took place. This part helps the interviewer understand the context of your story.

- **Example**: "In my previous role as a project manager at XYZ Company, we were tasked with launching a new product within a tight deadline."

1. **Task** Next, outline the specific task or challenge you faced in that situation. What was your responsibility? This step is crucial for clarifying your role in the story and highlighting the significance of the task at hand.

- **Example**: "My responsibility was to coordinate the efforts of the marketing, sales, and development teams to ensure that the product was launched on time and met our quality standards."

1. **Action** Describe the actions you took to address the situation and complete the task. This is where you showcase your skills and decision-making process. Focus on your contributions, even if you were part of a team. Be specific about what you did, highlighting your thought process and problem-solving abilities.

- **Example**: "I organized weekly meetings with all stakeholders to track progress, address any roadblocks, and ensure alignment. I also implemented a shared project management tool to enhance collaboration and transparency."

1. **Result** Finally, discuss the outcome of your actions. What were the results? Quantify your achievements whenever possible. This is your opportunity to demonstrate the impact of your work and show how you added value to the organization.

- **Example**: "As a result, we successfully launched the product two weeks ahead of schedule, which led to a 30% increase in initial sales compared to our projections and positive feedback from our customers."

1. **Practice Using STAR** To become comfortable using the STAR method, practice responding to common behavioral questions. Write down potential questions and formulate your answers using the STAR structure. This preparation will help you deliver confident and well-organized responses during interviews.
2. **Adapting to Different Contexts** While the STAR method is primarily used for behavioral questions, you can adapt its structure for technical questions as well. For example, when discussing a technical challenge, outline the situation, the task at hand, the technical steps you took, and the outcome. This approach ensures that your technical expertise is

CHAPTER 4: ANTICIPATING COMMON INTERVIEW QUESTIONS

communicated clearly.

3. **Using Follow-Up Questions** Be prepared for follow-up questions after your STAR responses. Interviewers may want to dig deeper into your experiences, so stay flexible and ready to provide additional details or examples. This further demonstrates your ability to reflect on your experiences and communicate effectively.

By mastering the STAR method, you will enhance your ability to articulate your experiences in a structured and compelling manner, making it easier for interviewers to understand your qualifications and fit for the role.

Handling Situational Questions

Situational questions are designed to assess how you would handle hypothetical scenarios that may arise in the workplace. Unlike behavioral questions, which focus on past experiences, situational questions require you to think critically and demonstrate your problem-solving skills.

1. **Understand the Purpose** Situational questions help interviewers gauge your thought process, judgment, and ability to navigate challenges. They may present you with a specific scenario related to the job and ask how you would respond.

- **Examples of Situational Questions**:
- "What would you do if you were assigned a project with an unrealistic deadline?"
- "How would you handle a disagreement with a team member?"
- "If a client expressed dissatisfaction with your work, how would you address it?"

1. **Approach with the STAR Method** Although situational questions are hypothetical, you can still use the STAR method to structure your responses. Begin by describing the situation you envision, the task involved, the actions you would take, and the desired outcome.
2. **Think Aloud** When answering situational questions, it can be helpful

to think aloud. Walk the interviewer through your thought process as you consider the scenario. This not only demonstrates your problem-solving abilities but also shows your reasoning and decision-making skills.

- **Example**: "If I were given an unrealistic deadline, I would first assess the project's requirements and the resources available. I would then communicate with my supervisor to discuss the feasibility of the timeline and propose adjustments if necessary."

1. **Emphasize Collaboration** Many situational questions involve teamwork or collaboration. Emphasize your willingness to work with others to resolve conflicts or challenges. Highlight how you value input from teammates and are open to finding solutions together.

- **Example**: "If I encountered a disagreement with a team member, I would first seek to understand their perspective by engaging in an open dialogue. I believe that collaborating on a solution that considers both viewpoints is crucial for maintaining a positive team dynamic."

1. **Stay Positive and Constructive** Even when faced with challenging scenarios, approach your answers with a positive and constructive attitude. Focus on how you would handle the situation effectively rather than dwelling on potential negatives.
2. **Use Real-Life Examples as Reference** If you have encountered similar situations in your past work experience, share those examples to illustrate your approach. While the questions may be hypothetical, your real-life experiences can lend credibility to your responses.

- **Example**: "In a previous role, I faced a situation where a client was unhappy with our deliverables. I scheduled a meeting to listen to their concerns and worked collaboratively with my team to make adjustments that addressed their feedback. Ultimately, this led to a

CHAPTER 4: ANTICIPATING COMMON INTERVIEW QUESTIONS

stronger relationship and positive outcomes."

1. **Practice Common Scenarios** Anticipate potential situational questions related to the job and practice your responses. Reflect on scenarios specific to your field, and prepare thoughtful answers that demonstrate your critical thinking and problem-solving abilities.

By effectively handling situational questions, you can showcase your ability to think on your feet and address challenges in a professional manner. This skill is essential for success in any workplace.

Most Common Behavioral Questions and Sample Answers

Familiarizing yourself with common behavioral questions and crafting sample answers can greatly enhance your interview preparedness. Below are several frequently asked behavioral questions along with examples of how to answer them effectively.

1. **Question: "Tell me about a time when you faced a significant challenge at work."**

   - **Sample Answer**: "In my previous role as a sales representative, I encountered a significant challenge when our primary supplier faced production delays. This resulted in our inability to fulfill customer orders on time. To address this, I organized an emergency meeting with our team to brainstorm solutions. We decided to reach out to alternative suppliers while keeping our customers informed about the situation. Through effective communication and negotiation, we secured a temporary supplier, allowing us to fulfill orders within two weeks. This proactive approach not only minimized customer dissatisfaction but also strengthened our relationships with clients."

1. **Question: "Describe a time when you had to work with a difficult team member."**

- **Sample Answer:** "In a group project during my last semester of college, I was paired with a team member who had a very different working style. They often missed deadlines and were resistant to feedback. I approached the situation by first having an open conversation with them to understand their perspective. I learned they were struggling with time management. I suggested we create a shared timeline with clear deadlines and agreed to check in regularly to provide support. This collaboration improved our communication and helped us successfully complete the project ahead of schedule."

1. **Question:** "Give me an example of a goal you set and how you achieved it."

- **Sample Answer:** "Last year, I set a goal to increase my sales by 20% within six months. To achieve this, I analyzed my current strategies and identified areas for improvement. I sought feedback from my manager and colleagues, which helped me refine my approach. I implemented a new customer relationship management tool to track leads more effectively and started networking with potential clients through industry events. By the end of the six months, I exceeded my goal, achieving a 25% increase in sales, which contributed significantly to our team's overall performance."

1. **Question:** "Tell me about a time when you had to adapt to change."

- **Sample Answer:** "During my tenure as a marketing coordinator, our company underwent a major rebranding initiative. This meant a complete overhaul of our marketing materials and strategy. I quickly adapted by diving into market research to understand our new audience. I collaborated with the design team to create fresh branding assets and developed a new content strategy that resonated with our target market. Despite the tight timeline, we launched the rebranding campaign on schedule, resulting in a 30% increase in engagement on our digital platforms."

1. **Question: "How do you handle tight deadlines?"**

- **Sample Answer**: "In my previous job as an event planner, I often faced tight deadlines. One particular instance involved organizing a corporate event with only three weeks' notice. To handle the pressure, I immediately created a detailed timeline outlining all tasks and deadlines. I delegated responsibilities to my team based on their strengths and established daily check-ins to monitor progress. By staying organized and communicating openly with my team, we successfully executed the event, which received positive feedback from both the attendees and the client."

1. **Question: "Describe a time when you took the initiative."**

- **Sample Answer**: "In my last position as a customer service representative, I noticed that our response times were slower than industry standards. Recognizing the impact on customer satisfaction, I proposed a new system for prioritizing urgent requests. I created a flowchart that outlined our process and presented it to management, along with data highlighting the potential benefits. Once implemented, our team reduced response times by 40%, leading to higher customer satisfaction ratings and positive feedback."

By preparing for these common behavioral questions and crafting thoughtful responses, you can present yourself as a capable and confident candidate during interviews.

Dealing with Unexpected or Curveball Questions

Unexpected or curveball questions can catch even the most prepared candidates off guard. These questions are often designed to assess your ability to think critically, problem-solve under pressure, and showcase your creativity. Here's how to handle them effectively:

1. **Stay Calm and Collected** When faced with an unexpected question, take a moment to collect your thoughts. It's perfectly acceptable to pause before answering, as this shows you are taking the question seriously. Deep breaths can help calm any nerves.
2. **Clarify the Question** If you don't understand the question, don't hesitate to ask for clarification. This shows that you are engaged and willing to ensure you address the interviewer's inquiry accurately.
3. **Use a Structured Approach** Just as you would with more traditional questions, use a structured approach to organize your thoughts. You can employ the STAR method or simply outline your reasoning. This organization can help convey your answer more clearly.
4. **Think Aloud** When answering, think aloud to demonstrate your thought process. This can be particularly effective for problem-solving questions. Walk the interviewer through your reasoning as you arrive at your answer.

- **Example**: "If I were to prioritize tasks with tight deadlines, I would first assess the urgency and importance of each task. I would consider factors like client expectations, project impact, and resource availability. Based on that assessment, I would tackle the most critical tasks first while ensuring I allocate time for any potential obstacles that might arise."

1. **Be Honest and Authentic** If you genuinely don't know the answer to a question, it's okay to admit it. Instead, share how you would approach finding the answer or solving the problem. This shows that you are resourceful and willing to seek solutions.

- **Example**: "I'm not familiar with that specific software, but I would start by reviewing the documentation and seeking tutorials online. I believe that learning new tools is essential, and I have a strong ability to adapt and pick up new technologies quickly."

1. **Maintain a Positive Attitude** Approach curveball questions with a

CHAPTER 4: ANTICIPATING COMMON INTERVIEW QUESTIONS

positive mindset. Emphasize your willingness to tackle challenges and learn from new experiences. This demonstrates resilience and adaptability—qualities that employers value.
2. **Practice with Friends or Mentors** To build confidence in handling unexpected questions, practice with friends or mentors. Have them ask you random questions to simulate the pressure of an interview environment. This will help you become more comfortable thinking on your feet.
3. **Reflect and Learn** After your interviews, reflect on any unexpected questions you faced. Consider how you handled them and whether there are areas for improvement. This self-reflection will better prepare you for future interviews.

By mastering the art of handling unexpected questions, you will enhance your ability to navigate interviews with confidence and poise. This skill not only showcases your adaptability but also your ability to think critically under pressure.

Anticipating common interview questions is a critical component of successful interview preparation. By understanding the differences between behavioral and technical questions, utilizing the STAR method for structured responses, handling situational inquiries, and preparing for curveball questions, you can approach interviews with greater confidence. Through practice and reflection, you will refine your ability to articulate your experiences and demonstrate your value as a candidate. With these strategies in place, you will be well-equipped to ace every interview you face.

Chapter 5: Navigating Difficult Questions with Confidence

Job interviews can be daunting, especially when faced with challenging questions that might catch you off guard. However, navigating these difficult inquiries with confidence is an essential skill that can significantly enhance your performance during interviews. In this chapter, we will explore some of the most common tough questions interviewers pose, including how to handle inquiries about weaknesses, salary expectations, employment gaps, conflicts, failures, and feedback. By mastering these responses, you'll be able to approach your next interview with poise and assurance.

How to Handle "What's Your Biggest Weakness?"

The question, "What's your biggest weakness?" can strike fear into even the most seasoned candidates. However, with the right approach, you can turn this question into an opportunity to demonstrate self-awareness, honesty, and a commitment to personal growth.

1. Understand the Purpose of the Question

Interviewers ask about weaknesses not to catch you off guard, but to assess your self-awareness and honesty. They want to see if you can reflect on your performance and acknowledge areas for improvement. Additionally, they may be looking for your strategies for overcoming challenges.

2. Choose a Genuine but Non-Critical Weakness

When selecting a weakness to discuss, choose something genuine but not critical to the role you are applying for. Avoid clichés like "I'm a perfectionist" or "I work too hard," as these can come across as insincere. Instead, consider weaknesses that show you're aware of your growth areas while also demonstrating your efforts to improve.

Example: "One area I've been working on is public speaking. In the past, I found it challenging to present in front of large groups, which affected my confidence. To overcome this, I enrolled in a public speaking course and volunteered for opportunities to present in team meetings. While I still feel a bit nervous, I've seen significant improvement and have even led several successful presentations in the last year."

3. Emphasize Steps Taken to Improve

After discussing your weakness, shift the focus to what you have done to address it. Highlight specific actions you've taken to improve your skills or overcome the challenge. This demonstrates your proactive attitude and commitment to professional growth.

4. Keep It Brief and Positive

While it's essential to provide a thoughtful response, keep your answer concise. Avoid dwelling on the weakness itself and focus more on your development journey. End on a positive note, indicating that you are continuously learning and growing.

5. Practice Your Response

Prepare your answer ahead of time and practice it. This will help you deliver it smoothly and confidently during the interview. Practicing in front of a friend or family member can provide valuable feedback and make you feel more comfortable discussing your weakness.

Answering Salary Expectations Gracefully

Discussing salary can be uncomfortable, but it's a crucial part of the interview process. Here's how to navigate questions about salary expectations with grace.

1. Research Salary Ranges

Before the interview, research the salary ranges for the position you're applying for in your geographic area. Websites like Glassdoor, Payscale, and LinkedIn Salary Insights can provide valuable data on what similar roles pay. This research will help you set realistic expectations and prepare for negotiations.

2. Deflect the Question If Needed

If you're uncomfortable discussing salary early in the interview, you can gently deflect the question. You might say, "I'd like to learn more about the responsibilities and expectations of the role before discussing salary. Can you provide more information about the position?"

3. Provide a Range Instead of a Specific Number

When the time comes to discuss salary, provide a range based on your research rather than a specific number. This shows flexibility and allows for negotiation. Ensure that your range reflects your skills, experience, and market value.

Example: "Based on my research and the industry standards, I believe a salary range of $70,000 to $80,000 is appropriate for this role, given my experience and the value I can bring to your team. However, I'm open to discussing this further based on the overall compensation package."

4. Consider the Entire Compensation Package

When discussing salary, consider the entire compensation package, including benefits, bonuses, and opportunities for growth. This shows that you're interested in more than just the paycheck and are willing to negotiate based on the full value of the offer.

5. Practice Your Response

Prepare your response to salary questions in advance. Practice discussing your salary expectations with a friend or mentor to build confidence. By rehearsing, you'll be better equipped to handle the conversation smoothly during the actual interview.

Discussing Gaps in Employment or Career Changes

Gaps in employment or significant career changes can raise concerns for interviewers. However, with the right approach, you can effectively address these topics and demonstrate your readiness for the role.

1. Be Honest and Transparent

If you have gaps in your employment history, be honest about them. Whether you took time off for personal reasons, further education, or family obligations, acknowledge the gap without providing excessive detail. Transparency builds trust with your interviewer.

2. Focus on What You Learned

Rather than dwelling on the gap itself, focus on what you learned or how you grew during that time. Highlight any skills you developed, volunteer work you engaged in, or courses you completed. This shows that you remained proactive and committed to personal growth.

Example: "I took a year off to care for a family member, which allowed me to develop strong organizational and time-management skills while balancing multiple responsibilities. During that time, I also completed an online course in project management, which I believe will greatly benefit me in this role."

3. Discuss Career Changes Positively

If you're making a significant career change, emphasize your transferable skills and experiences. Highlight how your previous roles have equipped you with valuable insights and abilities that are relevant to the new position.

Example: "While my background is primarily in marketing, I've always had a passion for data analysis. In my last role, I collaborated closely with the analytics team to inform our marketing strategies. This experience sparked my interest in pursuing a career in data analysis, and I've since completed several relevant certifications to build my expertise."

4. Prepare for Follow-Up Questions

Be prepared for follow-up questions about your gaps or career changes. Anticipate what the interviewer might ask and practice your responses. This preparation will help you stay calm and collected during the conversation.

5. Maintain a Positive Tone

Throughout the discussion, maintain a positive tone. Focus on your enthusiasm for the new role and how your unique experiences make you a strong candidate. This positivity can help reassure the interviewer and

CHAPTER 5: NAVIGATING DIFFICULT QUESTIONS WITH CONFIDENCE

redirect their focus toward your qualifications.

How to Address Team Conflict or Failure Stories

Discussing past conflicts or failures can be challenging, but these experiences often provide valuable insights into your character and ability to grow. Here's how to navigate these topics effectively.

1. Choose Relevant Examples

When preparing to discuss team conflicts or failures, select relevant examples that showcase your problem-solving skills and ability to learn from mistakes. Avoid overly negative or critical stories that could reflect poorly on you or others.

2. Use the STAR Method

Utilize the STAR method (Situation, Task, Action, Result) to structure your responses. This approach helps you provide a clear and concise narrative that emphasizes your role and the outcomes of the situation.

- **Situation**: Briefly describe the context of the conflict or failure.
- **Task**: Explain your specific role in the situation and what was at stake.
- **Action**: Detail the steps you took to address the conflict or resolve the issue.
- **Result**: Share the outcome of your actions, including any lessons learned.

Example: "In my previous role, I was part of a team working on a major project. We encountered a significant disagreement regarding the project direction (Situation). As the team lead, I was responsible for ensuring we met our deadlines (Task). I organized a meeting to discuss our differing viewpoints and facilitated a brainstorming session where everyone could voice their opinions (Action). Ultimately, we reached a consensus that incorporated the best ideas from each perspective, and we completed the project ahead of schedule (Result). This experience taught me the importance of open communication and collaboration in resolving conflicts."

3. Highlight Learning and Growth

When discussing failures, focus on what you learned from the experience and how you applied those lessons in subsequent situations. This demonstrates your resilience and commitment to personal and professional development.

Example: "In my first role, I led a project that ultimately failed to meet its objectives due to poor planning. While it was disappointing, I took it as an opportunity to reflect on what went wrong. I sought feedback from my manager and took a project management course to strengthen my skills. Since then, I've successfully managed multiple projects, ensuring thorough planning and execution."

4. Stay Professional

Regardless of the circumstances surrounding the conflict or failure, maintain a professional demeanor throughout your response. Avoid placing blame on others or speaking negatively about colleagues. Focus on your actions and the positive outcomes that resulted.

5. Practice and Prepare

Rehearse your responses to potential questions about conflicts or failures. Practicing with a friend or mentor can help you gain confidence and refine your delivery. Familiarizing yourself with your stories will enable you to answer seamlessly during the interview.

CHAPTER 5: NAVIGATING DIFFICULT QUESTIONS WITH CONFIDENCE

Responding to Negative Feedback or Criticism Questions

Questions about negative feedback or criticism can feel uncomfortable, but they offer an opportunity to showcase your ability to accept constructive criticism and grow from it. Here's how to address these inquiries effectively.

1. Acknowledge the Value of Feedback

Begin your response by acknowledging the importance of feedback in professional growth. This sets a positive tone and shows that you view criticism as an opportunity for improvement.

Example: "I believe feedback is essential for growth and development. It allows me to gain new perspectives and continuously improve my skills."

2. Provide a Specific Example

When discussing a time you received negative feedback, provide a specific example that illustrates the situation. Describe the context, the feedback you received, and how you responded.

Example: "In a previous role, my manager provided feedback that I needed to improve my communication with team members. She noted that I often worked independently and didn't update the team on my progress. I appreciated her honesty and took it to heart."

3. Demonstrate Your Response and Growth

Explain how you responded to the feedback and what steps you took to improve. This showcases your ability to learn from criticism and adapt your behavior.

Example: "After receiving that feedback, I took the initiative to schedule regular check-ins with my team to share updates on my work and solicit their input. I also started using project management tools to keep everyone informed about our progress. As a result, my communication improved significantly, and my team felt more engaged in the projects."

4. Focus on Positive Outcomes

Conclude your response by highlighting the positive outcomes of your actions. Emphasize how the experience improved your performance and strengthened your relationships with colleagues.

Example: "My improved communication led to increased collaboration within the team and ultimately contributed to the success of our projects. I'm grateful for that feedback, as it taught me the value of staying connected with my team and keeping everyone informed."

5. Practice Your Response

Prepare your response to questions about negative feedback in advance. Rehearse with a friend or mentor to ensure you can articulate your thoughts clearly and confidently during the interview.

Navigating difficult questions in interviews requires preparation, self-awareness, and the ability to turn challenges into opportunities. By mastering how to handle inquiries about weaknesses, salary expectations, employment gaps, conflicts, and negative feedback, you will be well-equipped to approach interviews with confidence. Remember to be honest, focus on personal growth, and practice your responses to ensure a seamless delivery. With these strategies in your toolkit, you will be ready to tackle any tough question that comes your way, ultimately increasing your chances of success in securing the job you desire.

Chapter 6: The Body Language of Confidence

In the world of job interviews, what you say is only part of the equation. Your body language, which communicates your feelings and confidence, plays a crucial role in how you are perceived. Understanding and mastering body language can enhance your overall presentation, helping you convey calmness and assurance during interviews. In this chapter, we will delve into the various aspects of body language, including non-verbal cues, how to project confidence, the identification and correction of nervous ticks, and the importance of smiling and pausing in effective communication.

Mastering Non-Verbal Cues: Eye Contact, Posture, and Gestures

Non-verbal communication encompasses a variety of behaviors that convey your feelings, attitudes, and intentions. Mastering these cues is essential for projecting confidence during interviews.

1. Eye Contact

Eye contact is one of the most powerful non-verbal cues you can employ. It indicates attentiveness, confidence, and sincerity. Here are some tips on how to effectively use eye contact during interviews:

- **Establish Engagement**: Aim to maintain eye contact for about 50-70% of the conversation. This shows you are engaged and interested in the discussion. When speaking, make direct eye contact with the interviewer, but also remember to glance at others in the room to create a connection with the whole panel.
- **Avoid Staring**: While eye contact is important, avoid staring, as it can make others uncomfortable. Instead, practice a natural shift of your gaze, moving between the interviewer's eyes and other facial features (like the nose or mouth).
- **Respond to Cues**: Be attentive to the interviewer's body language as well. If they look away frequently, it may indicate disinterest. Adjust your eye contact accordingly to keep the interaction comfortable.
- **Cultural Considerations**: Keep in mind that cultural differences may influence eye contact. In some cultures, too much eye contact can be considered disrespectful, so be aware of the cultural context if you are interviewing in a diverse environment.

2. Posture

Your posture can convey a wealth of information about your confidence level. Here are some key tips for maintaining positive posture during an interview:

- **Sit Up Straight**: Good posture is essential for projecting confidence. Sit up straight with your shoulders back and your feet flat on the ground. This posture not only makes you appear taller but also conveys an air of authority.
- **Open Body Language**: Avoid crossing your arms or legs, as these positions can signal defensiveness or discomfort. Instead, keep your arms relaxed at your sides or use them to gesture naturally while speaking. Open body language indicates receptiveness and approachability.
- **Leaning In**: Lean slightly forward during the conversation to show interest and engagement. This subtle movement communicates enthusiasm and attentiveness without invading personal space.

- **Avoid Fidgeting**: Refrain from excessive movement, such as tapping your foot or playing with your hair. Such fidgeting can be distracting and may signal anxiety. Practice maintaining a relaxed, composed posture throughout the interview.

3. Gestures

Gestures can enhance your verbal communication and help convey your points more effectively. Here's how to use gestures to your advantage:

- **Natural Hand Movements**: Use your hands to emphasize points while speaking, but keep your gestures natural and controlled. Overly animated or erratic gestures can distract from your message. Aim for gestures that complement your speech, such as using your hands to illustrate a point or show enthusiasm.
- **Palm Up or Open Gestures**: Open gestures, such as showing your palms or keeping your hands in a relaxed position, signal honesty and openness. These gestures invite the interviewer into the conversation and create a sense of trust.
- **Avoid Pointing**: Pointing can be perceived as aggressive or confrontational. Instead, use your whole hand to gesture or indicate direction when appropriate.
- **Practice Gestures**: To become more comfortable with your gestures, practice speaking in front of a mirror or record yourself. This can help you become more aware of your natural movements and adjust them as needed.

How to Use Body Language to Convey Calm and Assurance

Displaying calmness and assurance through body language can significantly impact how you are perceived during an interview. Here are several techniques to help you achieve this:

1. Controlled Breathing

Your breath can greatly influence your body language. Practicing controlled breathing techniques can help you remain calm and centered during the interview:

- **Deep Breaths**: Take a few deep breaths before entering the interview room. Inhale deeply through your nose, hold for a few seconds, and exhale slowly through your mouth. This can help reduce anxiety and set a calm tone.
- **Breath Awareness**: During the interview, pay attention to your breathing. If you notice your breath becoming shallow, take a moment to consciously breathe deeper. This will help ground you and maintain a steady presence.

2. Mindfulness and Presence

Being present in the moment can enhance your confidence and calmness. Here's how to cultivate mindfulness during interviews:

- **Active Listening**: Focus on the interviewer's words and non-verbal cues, rather than worrying about your responses. This will help you engage fully and respond more naturally.
- **Visualization Techniques**: Before the interview, visualize yourself in a confident and successful scenario. Imagine yourself answering questions smoothly and maintaining positive body language. This mental rehearsal can help build confidence and reduce anxiety.

3. Control Your Speed and Tone

The speed and tone of your speech can convey confidence and assurance. Here's how to manage these aspects effectively:

- **Pace Yourself**: Speak at a steady pace rather than rushing through your answers. This conveys confidence and gives you time to think about your responses.
- **Modulate Your Tone**: Pay attention to the tone of your voice. Aim for a calm, steady tone that reflects confidence. Avoid speaking too softly, as this can be perceived as insecurity.

4. Positive Affirmations

Using positive affirmations can reinforce a confident mindset:

- **Internal Dialogue**: Before the interview, remind yourself of your strengths and accomplishments. Use affirmations such as "I am prepared and capable" or "I have valuable skills to offer." This positive internal dialogue can help boost your confidence.
- **Visual Cues**: Consider visualizing positive affirmations in your mind while preparing for the interview. This can create a sense of confidence and calm.

5. Use Mirrors to Practice

Practicing in front of a mirror allows you to see your body language and facial expressions. This feedback can help you adjust your non-verbal cues to align with a confident demeanor.

Spotting and Correcting Nervous Ticks

Nervous ticks can detract from your confidence and may signal anxiety during an interview. Identifying and correcting these behaviors is essential for projecting assurance.

1. Common Nervous Ticks

Familiarize yourself with common nervous ticks that may manifest during interviews:

- **Fidgeting**: This includes tapping your foot, playing with your hair, or shifting in your seat. Such movements can be distracting and convey nervousness.
- **Touching Your Face**: Constantly touching your face, such as rubbing your eyes or adjusting your hair, can indicate anxiety and may be perceived as unprofessional.
- **Crossing Arms or Legs**: Closed body language, such as crossing your arms or legs, can signal defensiveness or discomfort.

2. Self-Awareness and Observation

The first step in correcting nervous ticks is developing self-awareness. Here's how to identify your nervous habits:

- **Record Yourself**: Consider recording practice interviews to observe your body language. This can help you identify specific nervous ticks that you may not be aware of.
- **Seek Feedback**: Ask a trusted friend or mentor to observe your body language during practice sessions. They can provide valuable feedback and help you identify nervous habits.

3. Implementing Corrections

Once you identify your nervous ticks, practice implementing corrections:

- **Redirect Energy**: Instead of fidgeting, find a constructive way to redirect your energy. For example, you can place your hands on the table or in your lap, which provides a grounded position.

- **Practice Relaxation Techniques**: Incorporate relaxation techniques, such as deep breathing or mindfulness, into your preparation routine. This can help reduce anxiety and minimize the likelihood of nervous ticks.
- **Focus on Positive Posture**: Maintain an open and confident posture throughout the interview. Remind yourself to sit up straight and relax your shoulders, as this can help counteract nervous habits.

4. Build Confidence through Preparation

One of the best ways to combat nervous ticks is to build confidence through thorough preparation. When you feel prepared, you are less likely to resort to nervous habits.

- **Mock Interviews**: Conduct mock interviews with friends or family members. This practice can help familiarize you with common questions and allow you to develop confident responses.
- **Visualization**: Visualize yourself succeeding in the interview. Imagine yourself speaking clearly and confidently, without nervous ticks. This mental preparation can reinforce a sense of assurance.

The Role of Smiling and Pausing in Effective Communication

Smiling and pausing are powerful tools in effective communication. They can enhance your overall presence during interviews and create a positive impression.

1. The Power of Smiling

A genuine smile can significantly impact your body language and how others perceive you:

- **Conveying Approachability**: Smiling makes you appear more ap-

proachable and friendly. This invites the interviewer to engage with you more openly.
- **Positive Association**: When you smile, it triggers the release of endorphins, which can create a sense of positivity and reduce your own anxiety. This not only benefits you but can also uplift the mood of the interviewer.
- **Practice Your Smile**: Before the interview, practice your smile in front of a mirror to ensure it feels natural. A forced smile can come across as insincere, so focus on cultivating a genuine expression.

2. Effective Pausing

Pausing strategically during your responses can enhance your communication:

- **Allow Time for Reflection**: Pauses give you time to gather your thoughts and formulate clear responses. This can prevent you from rushing through answers and appearing anxious.
- **Emphasizing Points**: Use pauses to emphasize key points in your responses. This draws attention to important information and allows the interviewer to absorb what you are saying.
- **Avoiding Filler Words**: By incorporating pauses, you can reduce the use of filler words such as "um" or "like." This contributes to a more polished and confident delivery.

3. Balancing Smiling and Pausing

Striking a balance between smiling and pausing is essential for effective communication:

- **Smile When Appropriate**: Use smiles during introductions, when discussing positive experiences, or when expressing gratitude. This conveys warmth and positivity.

- **Pause for Effect**: When addressing more serious topics or questions, allow for pauses. This demonstrates thoughtfulness and confidence in your responses.

Mastering body language is a vital component of interview success. By focusing on non-verbal cues such as eye contact, posture, and gestures, you can project confidence and assurance. Learning to convey calmness through controlled breathing, mindfulness, and positive affirmations will further enhance your presence. Spotting and correcting nervous ticks is essential for presenting yourself authentically, while smiling and pausing contribute to effective communication.

With these strategies in your arsenal, you will be better equipped to navigate the interview landscape with confidence. Remember that body language is a reflection of your mindset, and by mastering it, you will not only feel more assured but also leave a lasting impression on your interviewers. Embrace the power of body language, and let it enhance your journey from nervous to confident during every interview you face.

Chapter 7: Building Rapport with Your Interviewer

Building rapport with your interviewer is a crucial yet often overlooked aspect of the interview process. Establishing a genuine connection can significantly enhance your chances of leaving a lasting impression, increasing your likelihood of success. This chapter explores the power of small talk, mirroring techniques, the role of active listening in connection, and the delicate balance between professionalism and approachability.

The Power of Small Talk: How to Break the Ice

Small talk serves as the foundation for building rapport during an interview. It creates a comfortable atmosphere and helps ease any tension, allowing both parties to engage in a more relaxed manner.

1. Why Small Talk Matters

Small talk may seem trivial, but it plays a vital role in establishing a positive connection:

- **Humanizing the Interaction**: Small talk humanizes the interview process, transforming it from a formal Q&A session into a more personal conversation. This sets the tone for open communication.

CHAPTER 7: BUILDING RAPPORT WITH YOUR INTERVIEWER

- **Easing Anxiety**: Engaging in light conversation can help reduce anxiety for both the candidate and the interviewer. It creates a friendly environment where both parties can feel at ease.
- **Creating a Lasting Impression**: Effective small talk can leave a lasting impression. A positive, relaxed interaction can make you memorable in the eyes of the interviewer.

2. *Topics for Small Talk*

Identifying suitable topics for small talk is essential for breaking the ice effectively:

- **Weather and Location**: Starting with neutral topics like the weather can be a safe choice. For example, "It's a beautiful day outside. Have you been able to enjoy it?"
- **Recent News**: Commenting on current events, particularly those relevant to the industry or company, can showcase your knowledge and interest. However, be cautious of sensitive topics.
- **Company Culture**: Inquiring about the company culture or recent developments within the organization can demonstrate your enthusiasm for the role. For example, "I read about your recent community service initiatives. How has the team been involved?"
- **Common Interests**: If you notice anything in the interviewer's background or office decor that suggests common interests (e.g., books, sports, or hobbies), use this as a springboard for conversation.

3. *Transitioning to the Formal Interview*

Once you've established rapport through small talk, transition into the formal part of the interview:

- **Use a Natural Flow**: After a few moments of small talk, smoothly transition by saying something like, "I really enjoyed our chat. I'm looking

forward to discussing how my experience aligns with this role."
- **Be Mindful of Timing**: Pay attention to the interviewer's cues. If they seem eager to dive into the formalities, be respectful and shift gears accordingly.

4. Practice Makes Perfect

Practicing small talk in various settings can improve your comfort level:

- **Mock Interviews**: Conduct mock interviews with friends or family, incorporating small talk into your practice sessions. This will help you become more adept at breaking the ice.
- **Social Settings**: Engage in small talk during social gatherings or networking events. This will refine your conversational skills and boost your confidence.

Mirroring Techniques: Aligning with Your Interviewer's Style

Mirroring involves subtly mimicking the interviewer's verbal and non-verbal communication styles. This technique can create a sense of connection and rapport.

1. Understanding Mirroring

Mirroring can be a powerful tool for building rapport:

- **Subconscious Connection**: People tend to feel more comfortable with others who exhibit similar behaviors. Mirroring can foster this unconscious bond.
- **Enhancing Communication**: When you align your communication style with the interviewer's, it can enhance understanding and reduce miscommunication.

CHAPTER 7: BUILDING RAPPORT WITH YOUR INTERVIEWER

2. How to Effectively Mirror

Here are some strategies for effective mirroring:

- **Observe and Adapt**: Pay attention to the interviewer's body language, tone of voice, and pacing. If they speak slowly, adjust your speech to match their rhythm.
- **Match Non-Verbal Cues**: Subtly mimic the interviewer's gestures and posture. If they lean forward, consider doing the same. However, be careful not to overdo it; the mirroring should feel natural and effortless.
- **Reflect Their Tone and Language**: If the interviewer uses formal language, respond in kind. Conversely, if they adopt a more casual tone, feel free to relax your language as well.
- **Be Genuine**: Mirroring should come naturally. Avoid forced mimicry, as it can come across as insincere. Authenticity is key to building genuine rapport.

3. Recognizing Boundaries

While mirroring can enhance rapport, it's essential to recognize boundaries:

- **Respect Personal Space**: Be mindful of the interviewer's personal space. Avoid invading their comfort zone while mirroring their body language.
- **Avoid Over-Mirroring**: Excessive mirroring can be perceived as mocking. Keep your adjustments subtle and harmonious.

How to Use Active Listening to Connect

Active listening is an essential skill for building rapport during an interview. It involves fully engaging with the interviewer and demonstrating your interest in what they are saying.

1. The Importance of Active Listening

Active listening helps create a deeper connection and enhances communication:

- **Demonstrating Respect**: By actively listening, you show the interviewer that you value their input and perspective. This respect fosters a positive rapport.
- **Enhancing Understanding**: Active listening allows you to grasp the nuances of the conversation. This understanding enables you to respond more thoughtfully and engage more meaningfully.

2. Techniques for Active Listening

Implementing effective active listening techniques can enhance your rapport-building efforts:

- **Maintain Eye Contact**: As discussed earlier, maintaining eye contact signals attentiveness. It shows that you are fully engaged in the conversation.
- **Use Verbal Affirmations**: Incorporate verbal affirmations such as "I see," "That's interesting," or "I understand" to demonstrate your engagement. These affirmations encourage the interviewer to share more.
- **Paraphrase and Summarize**: Reflecting on what the interviewer has said by paraphrasing or summarizing can enhance connection. For example, "So, you're saying that the company values collaboration. That resonates with my experience in team environments."
- **Ask Follow-Up Questions**: Pose relevant follow-up questions to deepen the conversation. This shows your genuine interest and encourages the interviewer to elaborate on their points.

3. Avoiding Distractions

Active listening requires focus. Here's how to avoid distractions during the interview:

- **Minimize External Distractions**: Ensure that your phone is silenced, and avoid fiddling with items on the table. Create an environment that allows you to concentrate on the conversation.
- **Stay Mentally Present**: Remind yourself to stay present in the moment. If your mind wanders, gently redirect your focus back to the interviewer.

4. Demonstrating Empathy

Empathy is a crucial component of active listening:

- **Acknowledge Feelings**: If the interviewer shares a challenging experience or concern, acknowledge their feelings with empathetic responses. For example, "That sounds like a challenging situation. How did you navigate it?"
- **Relate Your Experiences**: If appropriate, share relevant experiences that relate to the interviewer's sentiments. This creates a sense of shared understanding and strengthens your connection.

Balancing Professionalism and Approachability

Striking a balance between professionalism and approachability is vital for building rapport. You want to convey your competence while also making the interviewer feel comfortable engaging with you.

1. Establishing Professionalism

Professionalism sets the tone for the interview:

- **Dress Appropriately**: Ensure that your attire aligns with the company culture. Dressing appropriately conveys respect for the interview process and the organization.
- **Be Punctual**: Arriving on time demonstrates reliability and commitment. It establishes a professional first impression.
- **Maintain Polite Language**: Use courteous and respectful language throughout the interview. This shows professionalism and a serious attitude toward the opportunity.

2. Exuding Approachability

While professionalism is essential, approachability helps foster rapport:

- **Smile Genuinely**: A genuine smile can create an inviting atmosphere. It signals that you are friendly and open to conversation.
- **Use a Warm Tone**: Your tone of voice can impact how approachable you seem. Aim for a warm and friendly tone, even when discussing serious topics.
- **Share Personal Insights**: Offering a glimpse into your personality can enhance approachability. Share relevant personal anecdotes or insights that relate to the conversation.

3. Navigating Humor

Humor can be a double-edged sword in interviews. Here's how to navigate it effectively:

- **Use Humor Sparingly**: If you choose to incorporate humor, do so sparingly and appropriately. Light, situational humor can create a relaxed

atmosphere.
- **Gauge the Interviewer's Response**: Pay attention to the interviewer's reactions. If they respond positively, you may continue with light humor; if not, pivot back to professionalism.

4. *Tailoring Your Approach*

Every interviewer is unique, so tailoring your approach is essential:

- **Read the Room**: Pay attention to the interviewer's body language and tone. Adjust your approach based on their responses. If they seem more formal, lean into professionalism; if they appear relaxed, feel free to be more approachable.
- **Be Yourself**: Authenticity is key. While you may adapt your style, be true to yourself. Genuine connections are built on authenticity.

Building rapport with your interviewer is a critical component of the interview process. By mastering small talk, employing mirroring techniques, practicing active listening, and balancing professionalism with approachability, you can create a positive connection that enhances your chances of success. Remember that interviews are not just about assessing qualifications but also about building relationships. By embracing these strategies, you will be well on your way to transforming your interviews into meaningful conversations that resonate with your interviewers.

Chapter 8: Overcoming Anxiety During the Interview

Experiencing anxiety during an interview is a common challenge that many candidates face. The pressure to perform well, coupled with the fear of judgment, can create overwhelming feelings of nervousness. However, with the right strategies and techniques, you can learn to manage this anxiety and present your best self. In this chapter, we will explore effective pre-interview rituals, breathing techniques and mindfulness practices, mental reframing methods to turn nerves into excitement, and strategies for handling moments of freezing during an interview.

Pre-Interview Rituals to Calm Nerves

Establishing a pre-interview ritual can significantly help in managing anxiety. Rituals create a sense of familiarity and control, allowing you to enter the interview with a calmer mindset.

1. Establishing a Routine

Creating a consistent routine before interviews can help signal your brain that it's time to prepare mentally and emotionally. Here are some elements to consider including in your routine:

- **Preparation:** Begin by gathering all necessary materials, such as your

resume, cover letter, and any notes you may have prepared. Ensure that everything is organized and easily accessible.
- **Positive Visualization**: Spend a few minutes visualizing a successful interview. Imagine yourself walking into the room confidently, answering questions clearly, and leaving a positive impression. Visualization can help reinforce a positive mindset.
- **Physical Activity**: Engaging in light physical activity, such as stretching, yoga, or even a short walk, can help release pent-up energy and reduce anxiety. Physical movement encourages the release of endorphins, promoting feelings of well-being.

2. Setting the Environment

Creating a calming environment can also enhance your pre-interview rituals:

- **Quiet Space**: Find a quiet space to mentally prepare. This could be your home, a coffee shop, or any place where you can focus without distractions.
- **Comfortable Attire**: Dress in attire that makes you feel comfortable and confident. If you feel good in what you're wearing, it can boost your self-esteem.
- **Soothing Elements**: Consider incorporating soothing elements such as calming music, essential oils, or aromatherapy to help create a relaxing atmosphere.

3. Engaging in Positive Self-Talk

The way you talk to yourself can impact your mindset. Use positive affirmations to counteract negative thoughts:

- **Prepare Affirmations**: Create a list of positive affirmations that resonate with you, such as "I am prepared and capable," "I can handle any question," or "I am confident in my abilities."

- **Repeat Affirmations**: Take a few moments to repeat these affirmations aloud or silently to yourself. This practice can help shift your focus away from anxiety and reinforce a positive mindset.

4. Limit Information Overload

While preparation is essential, overloading yourself with information can lead to anxiety:

- **Focus on Key Points**: Concentrate on a few key points you want to communicate during the interview. Trying to memorize every detail can create pressure and increase anxiety.
- **Limit Distractions**: Avoid excessive reading or reviewing of materials just before the interview. Instead, focus on relaxation techniques or engaging in a calming activity.

Breathing Techniques and Mindfulness Practices

Breathing techniques and mindfulness practices are powerful tools for managing anxiety. They help ground you in the present moment and promote a sense of calm.

1. Deep Breathing Exercises

Deep breathing exercises can help lower anxiety levels by slowing your heart rate and promoting relaxation:

- **Diaphragmatic Breathing**: Also known as abdominal breathing, this technique involves breathing deeply from your diaphragm rather than shallowly from your chest. Here's how to do it:
- Sit or stand in a comfortable position.
- Place one hand on your chest and the other on your abdomen.
- Inhale deeply through your nose, allowing your abdomen to expand while

keeping your chest still.
- Exhale slowly through your mouth, feeling your abdomen contract. Repeat this for several breaths, focusing on the rhythm.
- **Box Breathing**: This technique involves inhaling, holding, exhaling, and holding your breath in a structured pattern:
  - Inhale through your nose for a count of four.
  - Hold your breath for a count of four.
  - Exhale slowly through your mouth for a count of four.
  - Hold your breath for another count of four.
  - Repeat this cycle several times to promote relaxation.

2. Mindfulness Meditation

Mindfulness meditation can enhance your ability to remain present and calm during an interview:

- **Find a Quiet Space**: Choose a quiet space where you can sit comfortably without distractions.
- **Focus on Your Breath**: Close your eyes and focus on your breath. Notice the sensation of the air entering and leaving your body. If your mind begins to wander, gently redirect your focus back to your breath.
- **Acknowledge Thoughts**: Allow any anxious thoughts to come and go without judgment. Acknowledge them, but do not dwell on them. This practice can help create distance between you and your anxiety.

3. Grounding Techniques

Grounding techniques can help bring your focus back to the present moment when anxiety arises:

- **5-4-3-2-1 Technique**: This technique involves engaging your senses to ground yourself:
  - Identify **five** things you can see.

- Identify **four** things you can feel (e.g., the chair you're sitting in).
- Identify **three** things you can hear.
- Identify **two** things you can smell (or imagine the smell of).
- Identify **one** thing you can taste (or imagine a taste).
- **Physical Grounding**: Focus on the sensation of your feet on the ground. Feel the connection between your body and the earth. This practice can help you feel anchored and present.

4. Incorporating Mindfulness into Daily Life

Incorporating mindfulness into your daily routine can help reduce overall anxiety:

- **Mindful Moments**: Take brief moments throughout your day to practice mindfulness, such as focusing on your breath during a break or savoring the taste of your food while eating.
- **Mindful Walking**: Engage in mindful walking by paying attention to the sensation of your feet touching the ground and the rhythm of your breath as you move.

Mental Reframing: Turning Nerves into Excitement

Reframing your mindset can transform anxiety into excitement, allowing you to approach the interview with a positive outlook.

1. Understanding the Connection Between Anxiety and Excitement

Anxiety and excitement share similar physiological responses, such as increased heart rate and heightened adrenaline. Recognizing this connection can help you shift your perspective:

- **Physical Sensations**: Instead of interpreting the physical sensations of anxiety as fear, reframe them as excitement. Tell yourself that your body

is preparing for something exciting.
- **Language Matters**: Change the language you use when thinking about the interview. Instead of saying, "I'm so nervous," try saying, "I'm excited for this opportunity." This shift in language can influence your emotional state.

2. Visualizing Positive Outcomes

Visualization is a powerful tool for mental reframing:

- **Imagine Success**: Take time to visualize yourself succeeding in the interview. Picture yourself answering questions confidently, engaging with the interviewer, and leaving the room with a sense of accomplishment.
- **Create a Success Timeline**: Develop a timeline of successful outcomes from previous experiences, whether in interviews or other high-pressure situations. Reflecting on past successes can help reinforce your confidence.

3. Embracing the Challenge

Viewing the interview as a challenge rather than a threat can alter your perspective:

- **Growth Mindset**: Embrace the concept of a growth mindset, where you see challenges as opportunities for growth and learning. Recognize that every interview is a chance to refine your skills and gain valuable experience.
- **Reframe Failure**: Understand that not every interview will lead to a job offer, and that's okay. Each experience provides insights and lessons that can enhance your future performance.

4. Setting Positive Intentions

Setting positive intentions before the interview can reinforce your confidence:

- **Intention Setting**: Take a moment to set intentions for the interview. For example, "I intend to be present and engaged" or "I intend to share my experiences authentically." Focusing on your intentions can guide your mindset during the interview.
- **Affirm Your Abilities**: Remind yourself of your strengths and qualifications. Create a list of your skills and achievements that you can refer to before the interview. This affirmation reinforces your competence.

What to Do If You Freeze During an Interview

Freezing during an interview is a common experience, often triggered by overwhelming anxiety or unexpected questions. Knowing how to handle this moment can make a significant difference in your performance.

1. Acknowledge the Freeze

If you find yourself freezing during the interview, it's essential to acknowledge the situation:

- **Pause and Breathe**: Instead of panicking, take a moment to pause and take a deep breath. This allows you to regain composure and collect your thoughts.
- **Don't Overthink**: Avoid overanalyzing the freeze. Remind yourself that it's a normal response, and it doesn't define your abilities.

CHAPTER 8: OVERCOMING ANXIETY DURING THE INTERVIEW

2. Employing Transition Techniques

Using transition techniques can help you regain your footing during a freeze:

- **Ask for Clarification**: If you're caught off guard by a question, consider asking the interviewer for clarification. This buys you time to gather your thoughts and shows your willingness to engage.
- **Repeat the Question**: Repeating the question can give you a moment to process while demonstrating that you are actively engaged in the conversation.
- **Take a Moment**: If needed, you can say, "That's a great question. Let me take a moment to think about it." This gives you permission to pause without feeling pressured to respond immediately.

3. Redirecting Focus

Redirecting your focus can help alleviate the pressure:

- **Focus on Your Strengths**: Shift your focus to your strengths and how they relate to the role. Remind yourself of specific experiences or skills that are relevant to the conversation.
- **Use Positive Visualization**: Visualize yourself successfully answering the question. This can help build confidence and reduce anxiety.

4. Post-Interview Reflection

After the interview, take time to reflect on the experience:

- **Evaluate the Situation**: Consider what led to the freeze. Were there specific triggers or unexpected questions? Understanding the root cause can help you prepare for future interviews.
- **Celebrate Your Efforts**: Regardless of the outcome, acknowledge your efforts. Reflect on what went well and what you learned, and celebrate

your courage in facing the interview.

Overcoming anxiety during an interview is a multifaceted process that involves preparation, mindfulness, mental reframing, and effective strategies for handling unexpected moments. By establishing pre-interview rituals, practicing breathing techniques, reframing your mindset, and knowing how to respond if you freeze, you can approach interviews with increased confidence. Remember, interviews are not just evaluations; they are opportunities for connection and growth. With practice and the right mindset, you can transform your anxiety into confidence and leave a lasting impression on your interviewers.

Chapter 9: Managing Virtual Interviews with Confidence

In recent years, virtual interviews have become an integral part of the hiring process. The COVID-19 pandemic accelerated this shift, leading many companies to adopt remote interviewing as a standard practice. While virtual interviews offer flexibility and convenience, they also come with unique challenges. Understanding how to navigate these challenges can enhance your performance and help you make a positive impression. This chapter will explore strategies for optimizing your virtual interview space, looking engaged on camera, adhering to virtual etiquette, and avoiding common pitfalls.

Optimizing Your Space: Lighting, Sound, and Background

Creating a conducive environment for virtual interviews is crucial. The space you choose can significantly impact how you present yourself and how you are perceived by the interviewer. Here are key elements to consider:

1. Lighting

Lighting plays a vital role in how you appear on camera. Poor lighting can make it difficult for the interviewer to see your facial expressions, diminishing your ability to convey confidence and engagement.

- **Natural Light**: Whenever possible, position yourself in front of a window to take advantage of natural light. This soft, flattering light enhances your appearance and provides a warm, inviting ambiance.
- **Supplemental Lighting**: If natural light isn't an option, consider investing in a ring light or desk lamp. Ensure that the light source is in front of you, illuminating your face rather than casting shadows. Avoid overhead lighting that may create harsh shadows.
- **Test Your Lighting**: Before the interview, test your lighting setup by recording a short video of yourself. Review the footage to see how you appear and adjust the lighting as needed.

2. Sound

Clear audio is essential for effective communication during a virtual interview. Background noise can be distracting and hinder your ability to engage with the interviewer.

- **Choose a Quiet Location**: Select a space that is quiet and free from distractions. Avoid high-traffic areas and rooms where background noise (like loud appliances or conversations) might disrupt the interview.
- **Microphone Quality**: If possible, use an external microphone or headset to improve sound quality. Built-in microphones on laptops may not capture your voice clearly, especially if you are seated far from the device.
- **Test Your Audio**: Conduct a sound check prior to the interview. Record a test audio clip to ensure that your voice is clear and at an appropriate volume.

3. Background

Your background can convey a lot about your professionalism and attention to detail. A cluttered or distracting background can detract from your message and create a negative impression.

- **Clean and Professional**: Choose a clean, uncluttered space for your interview. Remove any personal items or distractions that could draw attention away from you.
- **Virtual Backgrounds**: If your environment isn't ideal, consider using a virtual background. Ensure that it is appropriate and not overly distracting. Many video conferencing platforms offer built-in backgrounds, or you can upload a custom image that conveys professionalism.
- **Personal Touch**: While it's essential to maintain professionalism, incorporating a personal touch can help build rapport. For example, a bookshelf or a piece of art in the background can reflect your interests without being distracting.

How to Look Engaged on Camera

Maintaining engagement during a virtual interview requires conscious effort. It's easy to appear disengaged or distracted on camera, so implementing strategies to convey attentiveness is essential.

1. Body Language

Your body language communicates your level of engagement and confidence. Be mindful of your posture and gestures throughout the interview.

- **Sit Up Straight**: Maintain an upright posture to convey confidence. Avoid slouching, as it may signal disinterest or lack of confidence.
- **Use Gestures**: Incorporate hand gestures to emphasize points and convey enthusiasm. However, be mindful not to overdo it; excessive movement can be distracting.
- **Lean In Slightly**: Leaning in slightly toward the camera can create a sense of connection with the interviewer. It signals that you are engaged and interested in the conversation.

2. Eye Contact

Making eye contact during a virtual interview can be challenging, but it's crucial for establishing rapport.

- **Look at the Camera**: Instead of focusing on the screen or your own image, direct your gaze toward the camera lens. This creates the illusion of eye contact with the interviewer.
- **Avoid Distractions**: Minimize distractions on your screen to maintain focus. If your platform allows, hide non-essential windows to help you concentrate on the interviewer.

3. Active Listening

Demonstrating active listening can enhance your engagement and strengthen your connection with the interviewer.

- **Nod and Respond**: Use nonverbal cues, such as nodding, to show that you are listening and engaged. Occasionally responding verbally with affirmations like "I see" or "That makes sense" can also enhance engagement.
- **Avoid Interrupting**: Allow the interviewer to finish speaking before responding. If you need to take notes, do so discreetly to avoid appearing distracted.

4. Practice and Preparation

Preparation is key to feeling confident and engaged during a virtual interview.

- **Conduct Mock Interviews**: Practice with a friend or family member using the same video platform. This can help you become more comfortable with the technology and gain feedback on your engagement.
- **Review Your Materials**: Familiarize yourself with your resume and any

CHAPTER 9: MANAGING VIRTUAL INTERVIEWS WITH CONFIDENCE

notes you want to reference. Being prepared allows you to focus on the conversation rather than scrambling for information.

Virtual Etiquette: Timing, Tech, and Politeness

Understanding and adhering to virtual etiquette can enhance your professionalism during the interview. From punctuality to tech readiness, every detail matters.

1. Punctuality

Being punctual is essential, even in a virtual setting. Arriving late can create a negative impression.

- **Log In Early**: Aim to log in at least 10-15 minutes before the scheduled start time. This allows you to address any technical issues and demonstrates your commitment to the interview.
- **Test Your Technology**: Prior to the interview day, test your technology to ensure everything is working correctly. This includes your internet connection, camera, microphone, and any software used for the interview.

2. Technical Preparedness

Technical difficulties can disrupt the flow of an interview. Being prepared can help you navigate these challenges effectively.

- **Familiarize Yourself with the Platform**: Whether it's Zoom, Microsoft Teams, or another platform, take time to familiarize yourself with the features and functionalities. Understanding how to share your screen, mute/unmute, and use the chat feature can enhance your experience.
- **Backup Plan**: Have a backup plan in case of technical issues. This might involve using a secondary device (like a smartphone) or having the

interviewer's contact information readily available in case you need to switch to a phone call.

3. Politeness and Professionalism

Professionalism and politeness are key components of virtual etiquette.

- **Introduce Yourself Clearly**: At the beginning of the interview, introduce yourself clearly and express gratitude for the opportunity. A simple "Thank you for having me" can set a positive tone.
- **Address the Interviewer Properly**: Use the interviewer's name and title appropriately. This shows respect and professionalism.
- **Mind Your Tone**: Be mindful of your tone and language throughout the interview. Speak clearly and professionally, avoiding slang or overly casual language.

4. Follow-Up Etiquette

Following up after the interview is a crucial part of virtual etiquette.

- **Send a Thank-You Email**: Within 24 hours of the interview, send a thank-you email to express gratitude for the opportunity. This reinforces your interest in the position and leaves a positive impression.
- **Personalize Your Message**: Reference specific points from the interview to personalize your message. This demonstrates your attentiveness and engagement during the conversation.

Avoiding Common Pitfalls in Video Interviews

Despite the advantages of virtual interviews, several common pitfalls can detract from your performance. Being aware of these pitfalls allows you to prepare effectively and avoid them.

CHAPTER 9: MANAGING VIRTUAL INTERVIEWS WITH CONFIDENCE

1. Technical Issues

Technical difficulties are among the most common challenges during virtual interviews.

- **Internet Connectivity**: A stable internet connection is crucial. If possible, use a wired connection instead of Wi-Fi to reduce the risk of interruptions.
- **Device Preparation**: Ensure that your device is charged and functioning properly. Close unnecessary applications that may consume bandwidth or slow down your device.

2. Distractions

Distractions in your environment can hinder your performance during a virtual interview.

- **Minimize Interruptions**: Inform anyone in your household that you will be interviewing and request minimal interruptions. Use a "do not disturb" sign if needed.
- **Silence Notifications**: Turn off notifications on your device and avoid using your phone during the interview. This helps maintain focus and minimizes distractions.

3. Appearance and Attire

Your appearance is still important in a virtual interview, even if you're not meeting in person.

- **Dress Professionally**: Dress as you would for an in-person interview. Professional attire conveys seriousness and respect for the opportunity.
- **Consider Bottom Half Attire**: While it may be tempting to dress casually on the bottom half, dressing fully in professional attire can help

maintain a confident mindset.

4. Failing to Prepare for the Virtual Format

Approaching a virtual interview with the same mindset as an in-person interview may lead to oversights.

- **Practice for the Format**: Conduct mock interviews specifically in a virtual format. This helps you adjust to the nuances of communicating through a screen.
- **Familiarize Yourself with the Environment**: Practice speaking and presenting in front of the camera to build confidence and comfort in your virtual environment.

5. Neglecting Engagement

As previously mentioned, maintaining engagement is crucial for a successful virtual interview.

- **Stay Focused**: Avoid multitasking or checking your phone during the interview. Maintain eye contact and stay present in the conversation.
- **Respond Thoughtfully**: Take a moment to formulate your answers rather than rushing. Thoughtful responses convey confidence and insight.

Navigating virtual interviews with confidence requires a unique set of skills and strategies. By optimizing your interview space, appearing engaged on camera, adhering to virtual etiquette, and avoiding common pitfalls, you can enhance your performance and leave a positive impression on your interviewers. Virtual interviews are not just a technological necessity; they offer an opportunity to showcase your adaptability, professionalism, and

CHAPTER 9: MANAGING VIRTUAL INTERVIEWS WITH CONFIDENCE

communication skills in a digital age. With preparation and practice, you can approach virtual interviews with the same confidence as in-person meetings, turning challenges into opportunities for success.

Chapter 10: Handling Group and Panel Interviews

In today's competitive job market, interviews often involve multiple interviewers, whether in the form of panel interviews or group settings. While this format can be daunting, it also presents a unique opportunity to showcase your skills and adaptability. This chapter will delve into strategies for effectively navigating group and panel interviews, ensuring you maintain focus, engage with multiple interviewers, and turn the experience into a chance to shine.

Staying Focused When Facing Multiple Interviewers

Group and panel interviews can feel overwhelming, especially when faced with multiple interviewers firing questions from different angles. Staying focused is key to presenting yourself confidently and professionally. Here are strategies to help you maintain your composure:

1. Prepare Mentally

Before the interview, take time to mentally prepare for the experience. Visualizing a successful interview can help reduce anxiety.

- **Practice Relaxation Techniques**: Techniques such as deep breathing, meditation, or visualization can help calm nerves before and during the

interview. Prior to the interview, practice deep breathing exercises to center yourself.
- **Set Intentions**: Establish clear intentions for the interview. Decide what key points you want to convey and remind yourself of your qualifications. Setting intentions can provide a sense of purpose and focus.

2. Establish a Connection

Making eye contact and establishing a connection with each interviewer can enhance your focus and engagement.

- **Scan the Room**: When you enter the interview space, take a moment to scan the room and acknowledge each interviewer with a smile or nod. This helps you establish a rapport and sets a positive tone.
- **Engage with Each Interviewer**: As questions are asked, consciously engage with the person speaking. By maintaining eye contact and nodding in acknowledgment, you create a connection that enhances focus and engagement.

3. Active Listening

Active listening is crucial in group and panel interviews. It not only helps you respond appropriately but also shows respect for each interviewer.

- **Listen Carefully**: Pay close attention to each question asked. Avoid formulating your response while the interviewer is speaking. Instead, focus on their words and tone to fully understand their inquiry.
- **Ask Clarifying Questions**: If you find a question unclear, don't hesitate to ask for clarification. Phrases like "Could you please elaborate on that?" not only ensure you understand but also demonstrate your engagement.

4. Take Notes

Taking notes during the interview can help you stay organized and focused.

- **Jot Down Key Points**: Use a notebook or digital device to jot down key points, questions, or insights during the discussion. This can serve as a reference when responding to questions.
- **Avoid Overloading Yourself**: While taking notes is beneficial, avoid writing down everything. Focus on capturing essential points that can help guide your responses.

How to Address Multiple People Without Losing Track

In group and panel interviews, addressing multiple interviewers can be challenging. However, with the right strategies, you can manage this effectively without losing track of the conversation.

1. Identify Each Interviewer

At the beginning of the interview, take note of each interviewer's name and role. This can help you address them appropriately throughout the conversation.

- **Use Name Tags or Introductions**: If name tags are available, use them as a reference. Alternatively, introduce yourself to each interviewer at the start and try to remember their names as they speak.
- **Refer to Interviewers by Name**: When responding to questions, incorporate the interviewer's name into your answer. For instance, "Thank you, Sarah, for that question; I believe…" This technique personalizes your response and keeps you engaged with each individual.

2. Segment Your Responses

Breaking down your responses can help you maintain clarity while addressing multiple interviewers.

- **Use a Structured Approach**: Organize your responses into segments. For example, when answering a multi-part question, briefly restate each part before addressing it. This helps keep the flow of conversation clear and allows all interviewers to follow along.
- **Summarize Key Points**: After responding, summarize your main points. This reinforces your message and helps clarify your response for everyone in the room.

3. Engage with the Group

Engaging with the entire group is essential in maintaining a sense of connection and focus.

- **Acknowledge All Interviewers**: Throughout your responses, make an effort to glance at all interviewers, not just the one who asked the question. This inclusive approach fosters a sense of engagement with the entire panel.
- **Encourage Dialogue**: If appropriate, invite other interviewers to chime in. Phrases like, "I'd love to hear your thoughts on this as well," can facilitate conversation and foster a collaborative atmosphere.

4. Practice Group Interviews

Prior to the actual interview, consider conducting mock group interviews with friends or colleagues.

- **Simulate Real Scenarios**: Invite several friends to ask you questions in a panel format. This practice will help you adapt to addressing multiple

people and improve your comfort level in group settings.
- **Request Feedback**: After your practice session, ask for feedback on your responses and engagement. Constructive criticism can help you refine your approach for the actual interview.

Strategies for Engaging Each Interviewer

Engaging multiple interviewers requires intentionality and adaptability. Here are strategies to ensure you connect with each interviewer during the conversation:

1. Adapt to Different Styles

Each interviewer may have a different communication style or personality. Adapting to these styles can enhance engagement.

- **Observe Body Language**: Pay attention to each interviewer's body language and demeanor. For instance, if an interviewer appears more formal, match their tone. Conversely, if someone is more relaxed, you can mirror that energy.
- **Tailor Your Responses**: Adjust your communication style based on each interviewer's preferences. If one interviewer asks technical questions, provide detailed responses. If another seems more interested in team dynamics, focus on your collaboration skills.

2. Encourage Interaction

Creating opportunities for interaction can help engage each interviewer and create a dynamic conversation.

- **Ask Questions**: At appropriate moments, ask interviewers questions that invite their input. For example, "How does your team approach project management?" This encourages dialogue and demonstrates your

CHAPTER 10: HANDLING GROUP AND PANEL INTERVIEWS

interest in their perspectives.
- **Seek Clarifications**: If an interviewer seems particularly engaged, ask follow-up questions to delve deeper into their insights. This not only demonstrates your interest but also fosters a collaborative atmosphere.

3. Share Relevant Experiences

When addressing questions, share experiences that highlight your qualifications and relate to the interests of the interviewers.

- **Connect Your Background**: Tailor your experiences to align with the interests of each interviewer. For example, if one interviewer is from the marketing department, emphasize your experience with marketing campaigns.
- **Provide Varied Examples**: When possible, share a variety of experiences that showcase different skills or perspectives. This approach keeps the conversation dynamic and relevant to all interviewers.

4. Practice Empathy and Active Listening

Empathy and active listening are essential in building rapport with multiple interviewers.

- **Acknowledge Perspectives**: Recognize and validate the perspectives of each interviewer. For instance, if one interviewer expresses a concern, acknowledge it by saying, "That's a valid point, and I appreciate you bringing it up."
- **Listen for Cues**: Pay attention to verbal and non-verbal cues from each interviewer. This can help you gauge their reactions and adjust your responses accordingly.

Turning Group Settings into an Opportunity to Shine

Group and panel interviews, while intimidating, can be transformed into opportunities for you to stand out as a candidate. Here are ways to leverage the format to your advantage:

1. Showcase Teamwork and Collaboration

Demonstrating your teamwork skills can set you apart in a group interview setting.

- **Highlight Collaborative Projects**: Share examples of successful team projects where you played a key role. Emphasize how you contributed to the team's success and highlight your ability to work well with others.
- **Discuss Conflict Resolution**: If applicable, share experiences where you navigated conflicts within a team. This showcases your ability to handle challenges and emphasizes your collaborative mindset.

2. Exhibit Confidence and Poise

Confidence is key in group interviews. Your demeanor can influence how interviewers perceive you.

- **Practice Positive Body Language**: Maintain an open posture, use appropriate gestures, and project your voice clearly. Confident body language enhances your credibility and makes you more approachable.
- **Stay Calm Under Pressure**: If faced with difficult questions or interruptions, remain calm. Take a moment to gather your thoughts before responding, demonstrating poise and composure.

3. Follow Up Effectively

Following up after the interview can reinforce your positive impression and leave a lasting impact.

- **Personalized Thank-You Notes**: Send personalized thank-you notes to each interviewer, referencing specific points from the conversation. This demonstrates your attentiveness and gratitude for their time.
- **Highlight Your Interest**: In your follow-up communication, reiterate your interest in the position and the company. Mention how you believe your skills align with the team's goals.

4. Reflect on the Experience

After the interview, take time to reflect on the experience. Assess what went well and what areas you can improve upon for future group settings.

- **Identify Strengths and Weaknesses**: Evaluate your performance, noting what aspects you excelled in and areas that could use improvement. This reflection can guide your preparation for future interviews.
- **Seek Feedback**: If possible, ask for feedback from trusted friends or mentors. They may provide insights that can help you refine your approach in future group interviews.

Handling group and panel interviews can be a challenging yet rewarding experience. By staying focused, effectively addressing multiple interviewers, engaging each individual, and leveraging the group setting to showcase your skills, you can navigate these interviews with confidence. Remember, preparation and practice are essential for turning these interviews into opportunities to shine, helping you stand out as a candidate and making a lasting impression on potential employers.

Chapter 11: Answering Behavioral Questions with Impact

Behavioral interviews have become a standard in the hiring process, allowing employers to assess how candidates have handled situations in the past. The premise is simple: past behavior is a strong indicator of future performance. Thus, mastering the art of answering behavioral questions is essential for candidates who want to leave a lasting impression. This chapter will guide you through the STAR method, provide tips on crafting memorable stories, highlight pitfalls to avoid, and offer examples of compelling behavioral responses.

In-depth Guide to the STAR Method

The STAR method is a structured approach to answering behavioral questions effectively. The acronym stands for **Situation**, **Task**, **Action**, and **Result**. This method helps you organize your thoughts and ensures that you convey relevant information succinctly.

1. Situation

Begin your response by setting the context for your story. Describe the situation you faced, providing enough detail to allow the interviewer to understand the background.

- **Be Specific**: Instead of generalizing, provide a clear scenario. For instance, instead of saying, "I worked on a project," you could say, "During my internship at XYZ Company, I was part of a team tasked with improving the efficiency of our customer service process."
- **Provide Context**: Explain the significance of the situation. What was at stake? This helps the interviewer grasp the importance of your actions.

2. Task

After establishing the situation, outline your specific responsibilities or the goals you were aiming to achieve. This part is crucial as it highlights your role in the context.

- **Define Your Role**: Clearly articulate what you were tasked with. For example, "My responsibility was to analyze customer feedback and identify key areas for improvement."
- **Set Goals**: If applicable, mention any quantifiable goals you aimed to achieve. This adds depth to your response and gives the interviewer a sense of the expectations.

3. Action

This is the core of your response, where you describe the steps you took to address the situation and accomplish the task.

- **Focus on Your Contributions**: Emphasize your actions, not the team's. Use "I" statements to highlight your contributions. For example, "I conducted a survey to gather customer insights and collaborated with the team to brainstorm potential solutions."
- **Be Detailed**: Provide enough detail to illustrate your thought process and the skills you utilized. However, avoid overwhelming the interviewer with too much information.

4. Result

Finally, conclude your response by discussing the outcome of your actions. This part is vital, as it showcases the impact of your efforts.

- **Quantify Achievements**: Whenever possible, include metrics to demonstrate your success. For example, "As a result of our efforts, customer satisfaction scores improved by 20% within three months."
- **Reflect on Lessons Learned**: If relevant, mention any lessons learned from the experience or how it influenced your future work. This shows your capacity for growth and reflection.

How to Make Your Stories Memorable

Crafting memorable stories is an art that can significantly enhance your responses to behavioral questions. Here are strategies to ensure your stories stand out:

1. Choose the Right Stories

Select stories that align with the job requirements and values of the company you're interviewing with.

- **Relevance is Key**: Prioritize stories that directly relate to the skills and attributes being assessed. For instance, if the role emphasizes teamwork, choose a story that highlights your collaborative efforts.
- **Variety of Experiences**: Prepare multiple stories that showcase different skills and experiences. This diversity enables you to adapt to various questions and circumstances during the interview.

CHAPTER 11: ANSWERING BEHAVIORAL QUESTIONS WITH IMPACT

2. Use Vivid Descriptions

Engage your interviewer by using vivid and descriptive language that paints a picture of the situation.

- **Sensory Details**: Incorporate sensory details to make your story more relatable. For instance, instead of saying, "We had a meeting," you could say, "In a bustling conference room filled with eager team members, we gathered to brainstorm solutions."
- **Emotional Engagement**: Connect with the interviewer emotionally by sharing your feelings during the experience. This adds depth to your story and helps the interviewer relate to your experience.

3. Incorporate a Narrative Arc

Structure your stories with a clear beginning, middle, and end to enhance engagement.

- **Set the Stage**: Begin by introducing the context and characters involved in the situation. This draws the interviewer into your story.
- **Build Tension**: Describe the challenges you faced and the stakes involved. This creates anticipation and keeps the interviewer engaged.
- **Resolve the Story**: Conclude with the resolution and the impact of your actions, reinforcing the positive outcome.

4. Practice, Practice, Practice

Rehearsing your stories is crucial to delivering them smoothly during the interview.

- **Mock Interviews**: Conduct mock interviews with friends or mentors to practice your storytelling. This helps you refine your delivery and receive constructive feedback.

- **Record Yourself**: Consider recording yourself while practicing your stories. Watching the playback can help you identify areas for improvement in your delivery and body language.

Avoiding the Trap of Over-Explaining

While it's essential to provide detailed responses, over-explaining can dilute the impact of your stories. Here are tips to avoid this trap:

1. Stay Concise

Aim for clarity and brevity in your responses. Focus on the most critical aspects of your story without unnecessary embellishments.

- **Practice Time Management**: Keep your answers within a reasonable time frame, ideally between 1 to 2 minutes. This ensures that you provide enough detail without overwhelming the interviewer.
- **Stick to the STAR Structure**: Adhering to the STAR method can help you stay focused and avoid veering off-topic.

2. Avoid Jargon

Using jargon or technical terms can alienate interviewers who may not be familiar with your field.

- **Use Simple Language**: Explain your experiences in straightforward language. This makes your story more accessible and ensures understanding.
- **Clarify When Necessary**: If you must use industry-specific terms, take a moment to clarify their meaning. This demonstrates your awareness of your audience.

3. Eliminate Unnecessary Details

While some context is important, avoid including irrelevant details that do not contribute to the core of your story.

- **Focus on Key Actions**: Concentrate on the actions you took and the results achieved. Extraneous information can distract from the main point of your story.
- **Edit Ruthlessly**: After crafting your story, review it critically and remove any unnecessary details. Aim for a streamlined narrative that conveys your message effectively.

4. Practice with Feedback

Getting feedback on your stories can help you identify areas where you might be over-explaining.

- **Seek Input from Others**: Share your stories with friends or mentors and ask them for their honest feedback. They can help you identify parts that may be too detailed or unclear.
- **Iterate Based on Feedback**: Use the feedback to refine your stories. Continuous improvement will help you develop concise and impactful responses.

Examples of Compelling Behavioral Responses

Here are some examples of compelling behavioral responses using the STAR method. These examples demonstrate how to structure your answers effectively while showcasing your skills and experiences.

Example 1: Handling a Difficult Team Member

Question: "Tell me about a time you had to deal with a difficult team member."
Response:

- **Situation**: "During a critical project at XYZ Company, I was part of a team working on a product launch. One team member consistently missed deadlines, which affected our progress."
- **Task**: "As the team lead, it was my responsibility to ensure the project stayed on track while maintaining team morale."
- **Action**: "I scheduled a one-on-one meeting with the team member to understand their challenges. During our conversation, I learned they were struggling with workload management. I offered to help them prioritize their tasks and suggested tools for better organization. Additionally, I communicated our deadlines to the entire team to foster accountability."
- **Result**: "As a result of our discussion, the team member improved their time management, and we successfully launched the product on schedule. The experience also strengthened our team dynamic and encouraged open communication."

Example 2: Overcoming a Challenge

Question: "Describe a time when you faced a significant challenge at work."
Response:

- **Situation**: "While working as a marketing coordinator, I was tasked with organizing our annual conference. A month before the event, our keynote speaker canceled due to a scheduling conflict."
- **Task**: "My task was to find a suitable replacement speaker and ensure the conference ran smoothly despite the setback."
- **Action**: "I quickly reached out to my professional network to identify

potential speakers. After conducting research and considering our audience's interests, I secured a well-known industry expert who agreed to speak on short notice. I also revised the marketing materials to highlight the new speaker and communicated updates to all attendees."
- **Result**: "The conference was a success, with positive feedback from attendees about the new speaker. Additionally, our team gained valuable experience in crisis management and adaptability, which we applied to future events."

Example 3: Leading a Successful Project

Question: "Can you share an experience where you led a successful project?"
Response:

- **Situation**: "In my role as a project manager at ABC Corp, I was assigned to lead a cross-functional team tasked with developing a new software feature that aimed to enhance user experience."
- **Task**: "My responsibility was to manage the project timeline, coordinate between departments, and ensure the feature met customer needs."
- **Action**: "I organized a kickoff meeting to establish clear goals and timelines. Throughout the project, I facilitated weekly check-ins to address any challenges and foster collaboration among team members. I also gathered feedback from users through surveys to ensure our development aligned with their needs."
- **Result**: "The new feature was launched ahead of schedule and received positive reviews from users, resulting in a 30% increase in user engagement. This success was recognized company-wide, and I was asked to present our process at the annual conference."

In conclusion, mastering the art of answering behavioral questions using the STAR method is vital for making a strong impression during interviews. By selecting relevant stories, using vivid descriptions, avoiding over-explaining, and practicing diligently, you can convey your experiences with impact.

Remember, your ability to articulate your past experiences will not only showcase your qualifications but also demonstrate your potential to contribute positively to the organization you hope to join.

Chapter 12: Demonstrating Leadership and Teamwork

In today's competitive job market, showcasing leadership and teamwork skills is essential for candidates seeking to differentiate themselves. Employers are not only looking for individuals who can work independently but also those who can contribute positively to group dynamics and demonstrate leadership qualities when necessary. This chapter will explore how to showcase leadership qualities without coming across as overconfident, discuss how to effectively communicate team contributions, navigate questions regarding conflict resolution, and provide examples of strong leadership and teamwork responses.

Showcasing Leadership Qualities Without Sounding Overconfident

When discussing leadership during an interview, the goal is to highlight your capabilities while maintaining humility. Overconfidence can be off-putting, so it's essential to strike the right balance. Here are strategies to effectively showcase your leadership qualities without appearing arrogant.

1. Use Humble Language

Your choice of words can significantly impact how your message is perceived. Instead of making sweeping statements about your leadership skills, focus on your experiences and the outcomes of those experiences.

- **Avoid Absolute Claims**: Phrases like "I am the best leader" can come off as boastful. Instead, say, "In my previous role, I had the opportunity to lead a project that taught me valuable lessons about teamwork and communication."
- **Emphasize Team Achievements**: Frame your leadership in terms of team success rather than personal accolades. For example, "By facilitating collaboration among team members, we were able to achieve our goals ahead of schedule."

2. Highlight Collaborative Leadership

Effective leadership often involves collaboration and support. Emphasizing your ability to lead while valuing others' contributions helps convey humility.

- **Focus on Inclusivity**: Discuss how you involve team members in decision-making. For example, "I always encourage my team to share their ideas during brainstorming sessions, which fosters creativity and ensures that everyone feels valued."
- **Mention Mentorship**: Talk about how you've supported others' growth rather than just your achievements. You could say, "I enjoy mentoring new team members and helping them develop their skills, which contributes to the overall success of the team."

3. Provide Context for Leadership Experiences

When sharing leadership experiences, context is crucial. Describe the challenges you faced and how you approached them without claiming sole credit for the outcomes.

- **Detail Your Role**: Explain your responsibilities within the team and how you facilitated group efforts. For instance, "As a project coordinator, I organized meetings and ensured everyone was on the same page, leading to improved communication."
- **Share Outcomes**: Discuss the results of your leadership in a way that reflects the team's efforts. For example, "Through our collective efforts, we reduced project completion time by 15%, showcasing our ability to work together effectively."

4. Be Open About Learning

Acknowledging that you're continuously learning and growing as a leader demonstrates humility and openness.

- **Share Growth Experiences**: Talk about challenges you faced and how they influenced your leadership style. For instance, "During a particularly challenging project, I realized the importance of active listening. Since then, I've made it a priority to ensure all voices are heard."
- **Invite Feedback**: Mention how you seek feedback to improve your leadership skills. You could say, "I regularly ask my team for feedback on my leadership style to ensure I'm supporting them effectively."

Discussing Team Contributions Effectively

While showcasing your leadership abilities is important, being able to discuss your contributions as a team member is equally crucial. Here are strategies for effectively communicating your team contributions during an interview.

1. Frame Contributions in the Context of Team Goals

When discussing your role in a team, always relate your contributions back to the team's overall objectives. This shows that you understand the bigger picture.

- **Use Collaborative Language**: Instead of saying, "I completed the project," frame it as, "I contributed to the project by collaborating with my teammates to identify key challenges and solutions."
- **Showcase Synergy**: Highlight how your contributions complemented the efforts of others. For example, "While my colleague focused on data analysis, I supported them by conducting research that informed our decisions."

2. Share Specific Examples

Concrete examples of your contributions help paint a clearer picture for the interviewer and demonstrate your value to the team.

- **Quantify Your Contributions**: If possible, include metrics to illustrate your impact. For example, "As part of the marketing team, I implemented strategies that increased our social media engagement by 30%."
- **Describe Your Involvement**: Go into detail about your specific actions and how they contributed to the team's success. For instance, "I took the lead in organizing our team's weekly meetings, ensuring everyone had the opportunity to share updates and challenges."

3. Acknowledge Others' Contributions

While it's important to discuss your role, recognizing the contributions of your teammates fosters a sense of collaboration and teamwork.

- **Mention Collaborators**: When discussing a project, mention other team

members and their contributions. For example, "Working closely with our graphic designer, we created a presentation that effectively conveyed our findings."
- **Show Appreciation**: Express gratitude for your teammates' efforts when discussing a successful project. You might say, "I'm proud of what we achieved as a team and grateful for the support of my colleagues throughout the process."

4. Demonstrate Flexibility and Adaptability

In team environments, flexibility is key. Discuss how you adapted to different roles or circumstances within the team to meet collective goals.

- **Highlight Versatility**: Talk about times when you stepped outside your usual role to support your team. For example, "When our team leader was unavailable, I stepped in to facilitate meetings and keep the project on track."
- **Emphasize Problem-Solving**: Discuss how you helped the team navigate challenges by being adaptable. For instance, "When we faced unexpected delays, I suggested alternative strategies that allowed us to meet our deadlines."

Handling Questions on Conflict Resolution

Conflict is an inevitable part of teamwork, and how you handle it can reveal a lot about your interpersonal skills and maturity. Here are strategies for effectively discussing conflict resolution in an interview.

1. Acknowledge Conflict as a Natural Process

Begin by recognizing that conflict is a natural occurrence in any team setting. This mindset demonstrates your understanding of group dynamics.

- **Normalizing Conflict**: You might say, "I believe that conflict can lead to productive discussions and better outcomes when managed effectively."
- **Contextualizing Your Experience**: Frame your conflict resolution experiences as learning opportunities. For example, "I encountered conflicts in the past, and they taught me the importance of open communication and empathy."

2. Use the STAR Method for Conflict Scenarios

When asked about a specific conflict, utilize the STAR method to structure your response.

- **Situation**: Briefly describe the context of the conflict. For instance, "During a project, two team members had differing opinions on the direction we should take."
- **Task**: Outline your role in the situation. You might say, "As the team coordinator, I felt it was my responsibility to address the conflict and facilitate a resolution."
- **Action**: Discuss the steps you took to resolve the conflict. For example, "I organized a meeting where each member could share their perspectives, encouraging respectful dialogue and understanding."
- **Result**: Conclude with the outcome of your actions. You could say, "As a result, we reached a consensus that combined both ideas, leading to a stronger project outcome and improved team cohesion."

3. Focus on Communication Skills

Effective communication is key to resolving conflicts. Emphasize how you utilize communication to navigate disagreements.

- **Active Listening**: Talk about how you practice active listening to understand different viewpoints. You might say, "I always ensure that everyone feels heard by actively listening and summarizing their points

before responding."
- **Empathy and Respect**: Highlight the importance of approaching conflicts with empathy. For example, "I strive to approach conflicts with an open mind and respect for each individual's perspective."

4. Demonstrate Follow-Up Actions

Conflict resolution doesn't end with a discussion; following up is essential for ensuring lasting harmony within the team.

- **Check-In**: Mention how you follow up with team members after a conflict has been resolved. For instance, "After the resolution, I made a point to check in with both team members to ensure they felt comfortable moving forward."
- **Promote Future Collaboration**: Discuss how you encourage collaboration after a conflict. You might say, "I believe in fostering an environment where team members can work together effectively, so I encouraged joint brainstorming sessions to strengthen their partnership."

Examples of Strong Leadership and Teamwork Responses

Now that we've explored how to effectively showcase leadership and teamwork, let's look at some examples of strong responses using the principles outlined in this chapter.

Example 1: Demonstrating Leadership

Question: "Can you describe a time when you took on a leadership role?"
Response:

- **Situation**: "In my previous role as a project manager at ABC Inc., our team was faced with an urgent deadline to deliver a software update."
- **Task**: "I was responsible for ensuring that our team met the deadline

while maintaining high-quality standards."
- **Action**: "I initiated a team meeting to discuss the project's status and reallocate tasks based on each member's strengths. I also implemented daily check-ins to monitor progress and address any issues promptly. Throughout the process, I encouraged open communication and offered support wherever needed."
- **Result**: "As a result, we completed the software update two days ahead of schedule, and the client praised us for our attention to detail and collaboration. The experience reinforced my belief in the power of teamwork and effective leadership."

Example 2: Discussing Team Contributions

Question: "How do you typically contribute to a team project?"
Response:

- **Situation**: "In a recent marketing campaign at XYZ Corp., our team aimed to boost our social media presence."
- **Task**: "My role involved coordinating the efforts of different team members and ensuring our messaging was cohesive."
- **Action**: "I facilitated brainstorming sessions, encouraging everyone to share ideas. I also collaborated with the design team to create visually appealing content that resonated with our audience. I regularly checked in with each member to provide support and gather feedback on our progress."
- **Result**: "The campaign led to a 40% increase in our social media engagement over three months. I believe our success stemmed from effective collaboration and clear communication among team members."

CHAPTER 12: DEMONSTRATING LEADERSHIP AND TEAMWORK

Example 3: Handling Conflict Resolution

Question: "Tell me about a time you dealt with conflict in a team setting."
Response:

- **Situation**: "During a group project in my marketing class, two teammates had differing opinions on our campaign strategy, which created tension."
- **Task**: "As the team leader, I needed to address the conflict to ensure our project stayed on track."
- **Action**: "I scheduled a meeting with both members to discuss their perspectives openly. I encouraged them to express their concerns and facilitated a respectful dialogue. By actively listening and summarizing their points, I helped them find common ground. Ultimately, we agreed to merge elements of both strategies, enhancing our overall approach."
- **Result**: "The project turned out to be one of the highest-rated in the class, and both teammates expressed appreciation for how the conflict was handled. This experience taught me the value of communication and empathy in resolving conflicts."

Demonstrating leadership and teamwork in an interview is crucial for making a positive impression on potential employers. By showcasing your leadership qualities through humble language, collaborative achievements, and effective conflict resolution, you can present yourself as a strong candidate. Remember to support your claims with specific examples, highlighting the impact of your contributions and fostering an environment of teamwork. In doing so, you'll not only demonstrate your skills but also your potential to thrive in any work environment.

Chapter 13: Closing the Interview with Confidence

The closing phase of an interview is just as crucial as the opening and the responses to questions. It's your last opportunity to leave a strong impression on your interviewers and reinforce your candidacy for the role. This chapter delves into effective strategies for closing the interview confidently, covering how to ask insightful questions, express your interest in the position, handle the "Do you have any questions for us?" moment, and the importance of sending thank-you notes afterward.

How to Ask Insightful Questions

Asking insightful questions during your interview not only shows that you are engaged but also allows you to gather valuable information about the role and the company. Well-crafted questions can also demonstrate your critical thinking skills and interest in the position. Here are some strategies for formulating and asking insightful questions.

1. Research the Company and Role

Before the interview, thoroughly research the company and the role you are applying for. This preparation will help you formulate questions that reflect your understanding of the organization and its needs.

- **Review the Company Website**: Familiarize yourself with the company's mission, values, products, services, and recent news. Understanding the company's goals can help you ask relevant questions.
- **Analyze the Job Description**: Look closely at the job description to identify key responsibilities and required skills. Craft questions that reflect your interest in these areas.

2. Focus on Company Culture and Values

Understanding a company's culture and values is essential for determining if it's the right fit for you. Ask questions that demonstrate your interest in the company's work environment and ethos.

- **Example Questions**:
  - "How would you describe the company culture here?"
  - "What qualities do you value most in your team members?"
  - "Can you provide an example of how the company supports professional development for its employees?"

3. Inquire About Team Dynamics

Questions about team dynamics can give you insight into how you would fit within the organization and what to expect from your potential colleagues.

- **Example Questions**:
  - "Can you tell me about the team I would be working with?"
  - "How does the team typically collaborate on projects?"
  - "What are some challenges the team is currently facing?"

4. Ask About Growth and Opportunities

Understanding potential growth opportunities within the company can help you gauge your career trajectory if you join the organization.

- **Example Questions**:
- "What opportunities for advancement exist within this role?"
- "How does the company support employees in achieving their career goals?"
- "What does success look like for this position in the first six months to a year?"

5. Explore Current Challenges and Goals

Demonstrating an understanding of the challenges the company faces can highlight your analytical skills and proactive nature. Asking about current challenges also allows you to align your skills with the company's needs.

- **Example Questions**:
- "What are the biggest challenges the team is currently tackling?"
- "Are there any upcoming projects or initiatives that you are particularly excited about?"
- "How does this position contribute to the company's overall goals?"

6. Avoid Generic Questions

While asking questions is essential, ensure they are not generic or easily answered through basic research. Avoid questions about salary or benefits at this stage unless the interviewer brings them up.

- **Instead of**: "What is the salary range for this position?"
- **Ask**: "Can you describe how performance is evaluated in this role?"

7. Be Attentive and Adaptable

Listen actively to the interviewer's responses and be prepared to ask follow-up questions. This shows your genuine interest and engagement.

- **Example**: If the interviewer mentions a recent project, you could ask, "What were some lessons learned from that project, and how might they influence future initiatives?"

The Right Way to Express Your Interest in the Role

Expressing your interest in the role is a critical part of closing the interview. It not only reinforces your enthusiasm for the position but also gives the interviewer an understanding of your motivation.

1. Be Genuine and Sincere

When expressing your interest, authenticity is key. Avoid using generic phrases that may come off as insincere. Speak from the heart and share specific reasons for your enthusiasm.

- **Example**: "I'm genuinely excited about this opportunity because I believe my background in project management aligns well with the goals of your team. I am particularly drawn to your commitment to innovation and teamwork."

2. Link Your Skills to the Role

Reiterate how your skills and experiences make you a strong fit for the position. By connecting your background to the role's requirements, you reinforce your candidacy.

- **Example**: "Based on our conversation today, I believe my experience in leading cross-functional teams and my ability to adapt to fast-paced environments make me well-suited for this role. I'm eager to bring my skills to your team and contribute to your projects."

3. Express Enthusiasm for the Company

In addition to showing interest in the role, demonstrate enthusiasm for the company itself. This shows that you are not only interested in the position but also in the organization's mission and values.

- **Example**: "I admire the company's dedication to sustainability and innovation. It resonates with my values, and I would be thrilled to contribute to a company that prioritizes these principles."

4. Use Positive Language

When closing the interview, choose positive and affirmative language. Words like "excited," "thrilled," and "eager" convey enthusiasm.

- **Example**: "I am excited about the possibility of joining your team and contributing to the innovative work being done here."

5. Be Prepared for a Follow-Up

Sometimes, interviewers may ask you directly if you are still interested in the position. Be prepared to affirm your interest confidently.

- **Example**: "Absolutely, I'm very interested in this role and the opportunity to be part of such a forward-thinking company. I believe I can make a meaningful contribution."

CHAPTER 13: CLOSING THE INTERVIEW WITH CONFIDENCE

Handling the "Do You Have Any Questions for Us?" Moment

The "Do you have any questions for us?" moment is a pivotal point in the interview. It's an opportunity to demonstrate your engagement and curiosity. Here's how to handle this moment effectively.

1. Prepare Questions in Advance

To make the most of this moment, prepare a list of thoughtful questions before the interview. This shows that you have done your homework and are genuinely interested in the company and the role.

- **Example**: "Yes, I have a few questions. I'd love to learn more about the team I would be working with and the projects currently in the pipeline."

2. Prioritize Your Questions

As the interview progresses, you may find that some of your questions are answered through the conversation. Prioritize your questions to ensure you ask the most relevant ones based on what you have learned during the interview.

- **Example**: If the interviewer has already discussed the team structure, you might skip that question and focus on another topic.

3. Stay Engaged and Adaptive

While asking your prepared questions, stay engaged in the conversation and be adaptable. If the interviewer mentions something interesting, feel free to pivot your questions to delve deeper into that topic.

- **Example**: "I noticed you mentioned the team's recent focus on innovation. Can you share more about how that approach has influenced your projects?"

4. End on a Positive Note

When you conclude your questions, express gratitude for the opportunity to ask them. This reinforces a positive impression and leaves a lasting impact.

- **Example**: "Thank you for answering my questions. It's been great to learn more about the company and the exciting work being done here."

Thank You Notes: The Final Step in a Strong Interview

Sending a thank-you note after your interview is a vital step in the process. It demonstrates your professionalism, reinforces your interest in the position, and gives you a chance to express gratitude for the opportunity. Here's how to craft an effective thank-you note.

1. Send It Promptly

Aim to send your thank-you note within 24 hours of the interview. This demonstrates your enthusiasm and professionalism.

- **Format**: Email is typically the preferred format for thank-you notes due to its speed. However, a handwritten note can make a lasting impression if appropriate for the company culture.

2. Personalize Your Message

When writing your thank-you note, personalize it by mentioning specific details from your conversation. This shows that you were engaged and attentive during the interview.

- **Example**: "Thank you for taking the time to speak with me today. I appreciated learning about your team's current project on [specific project discussed] and your insights into the company culture."

3. Reiterate Your Interest

Reaffirm your interest in the position and the company. This serves as a reminder of your enthusiasm and desire to contribute to the organization.

- **Example**: "I remain very excited about the opportunity to join your team and contribute to the innovative work being done at [Company Name]."

4. Mention Any Follow-Up Points

If there were any specific points you discussed during the interview that you would like to follow up on, mention them briefly in your thank-you note.

- **Example**: "I'd also like to follow up on our discussion about [specific topic]. I've thought more about how my background in [specific experience] could benefit your team."

5. Express Gratitude

Conclude your note by thanking the interviewer once again for their time and consideration.

- **Example**: "Thank you once again for the opportunity to interview for the [Position Title]. I look forward to hearing from you soon."

Closing the interview with confidence is an essential part of the job application process. By asking insightful questions, expressing your interest in the role and the company, effectively handling the "Do you have any questions for us?" moment, and sending a thoughtful thank-you note, you can leave a lasting impression on your interviewers. This final phase of the interview is your chance to reinforce your candidacy and demonstrate your professionalism, ensuring you stand out as a top candidate. With the right approach, you can transition from a nervous applicant to a confident, well-prepared candidate, ready to take the next steps in your career.

Chapter 14: Dealing with Rejection and Moving Forward

Experiencing rejection in the job interview process is a common yet painful aspect of seeking employment. Despite our best efforts, not every interview will result in an offer. However, how we handle rejection can significantly impact our future success. This chapter delves into strategies for dealing with rejection, turning setbacks into learning opportunities, seeking constructive feedback, building resilience, and using rejections to refine your approach.

Turning Rejections into Learning Opportunities

Rejection can feel disheartening, but it can also serve as a powerful catalyst for personal and professional growth. The key lies in how you perceive and respond to rejection.

1. Shift Your Mindset

Instead of viewing rejection as a personal failure, consider it an inevitable part of the journey toward finding the right job. Adopting a growth mindset can help you see rejection as an opportunity to learn rather than a setback.

- **Embrace the Learning Process**: Understand that every interview is a chance to enhance your skills and knowledge. Each experience brings

you closer to the role that truly fits your talents and aspirations.
- **Cultivate Self-Compassion**: Be kind to yourself in the face of rejection. Remind yourself that it's a universal experience shared by many successful professionals. Your worth is not defined by a single interview outcome.

2. Reflect on the Experience

After receiving a rejection, take time to reflect on the interview process. Consider the following questions to guide your self-reflection:

- **What went well during the interview?** Recognizing your strengths can boost your confidence for future interviews.
- **Were there any moments of discomfort or uncertainty?** Identifying these areas can help you target your preparation for future interviews.
- **Did you adequately showcase your skills and experience?** Assess whether your pitch was clear and aligned with the job's requirements.

By reflecting on your performance, you can identify areas for improvement while also reinforcing what you did well.

3. Create an Action Plan

Once you have reflected on the interview experience, develop a plan to address the identified areas for improvement. This could involve:

- **Practicing Interview Skills**: Engage in mock interviews to refine your responses and boost your confidence. Seek feedback from trusted friends, mentors, or career coaches.
- **Enhancing Skills**: Consider taking courses or attending workshops to fill any skill gaps. Investing in your professional development can increase your employability.
- **Networking**: Reach out to your professional network to gather insights about industry trends, potential job openings, and valuable advice on

navigating the job market.

4. Recognize the Value of Fit

Sometimes, a rejection indicates that the role or organization may not have been the right fit for you. Reflect on whether the job aligned with your values, career goals, and working style.

- **Identify Your Priorities**: Use this opportunity to clarify what you want in your next role. What aspects of the job or company culture are most important to you?
- **Use Rejection to Refine Your Search**: Knowing what you truly want can help you make more informed decisions in your job search moving forward.

How to Seek Constructive Feedback

Seeking feedback after a rejection can provide valuable insights that help you improve and grow as a candidate. However, approaching this task requires finesse and professionalism.

1. Timing Is Key

Reach out for feedback promptly after receiving the rejection. A timely request demonstrates your eagerness to learn and shows respect for the interviewers' time.

- **Example Timing**: Send an email expressing your gratitude for the opportunity and politely asking for feedback within a week of the rejection.

BRAVE AND PREPARED: ELEVATE YOUR INTERVIEW GAME

2. Craft a Thoughtful Email

When asking for feedback, compose a thoughtful and professional email. Here's a structure to guide you:

- **Subject Line**: Keep it clear and straightforward, such as "Thank You and Request for Feedback."
- **Greeting**: Address the interviewer by their name.
- **Express Gratitude**: Start by thanking them for the opportunity to interview and for their time.
- **Request Feedback**: Politely ask if they could share any insights on your interview performance.
- **Be Specific**: If there are particular areas you're curious about, mention them. For example, you might inquire about your technical skills or cultural fit.
- **Close Professionally**: Thank them again for their consideration and express your appreciation for any feedback they can provide.

Sample Email Template:

```
Subject: Thank You and Request for Feedback

Dear [Interviewer's Name],

I hope this message finds you well. I wanted to take a moment to
thank you for the opportunity to interview for the [Job Title]
position at [Company Name]. I enjoyed our conversation and
learning more about the exciting projects your team is working on.

While I am disappointed to learn that I was not selected for the
role, I am eager to improve and grow in my job search. If you have
a moment, I would greatly appreciate any feedback you could share
regarding my interview performance or any areas where I could
improve.
```

```
Thank you once again for your time and consideration. I wish you
and the team at [Company Name] all the best.

Sincerely,

[Your Name]
```

3. Be Open to Criticism

When you receive feedback, approach it with an open mind. Understand that constructive criticism is meant to help you improve.

- **Avoid Defensive Responses**: It's natural to feel defensive about your performance, but try to listen without taking it personally.
- **Ask Clarifying Questions**: If feedback is unclear, don't hesitate to ask for clarification. This shows your commitment to understanding and learning from the feedback.

4. Implement the Feedback

After receiving constructive feedback, take the time to analyze it and create an action plan. Consider how you can apply the feedback to future interviews.

- **Identify Actionable Steps**: Break down the feedback into specific steps you can take. For example, if feedback indicated you struggled with behavioral questions, focus on practicing those types of responses.
- **Track Your Progress**: Keep a journal of your interviews and the feedback you receive. This can help you identify patterns and track your improvement over time.

Building Resilience: Staying Positive and Persistent

Building resilience is essential for navigating the ups and downs of the job search process. Developing a positive outlook can help you persevere in the face of rejection.

1. Cultivate a Support Network

Surround yourself with supportive individuals who can uplift you during challenging times. This network can include friends, family, mentors, and fellow job seekers.

- **Seek Encouragement**: Share your experiences and seek encouragement from those who understand the job search journey.
- **Participate in Networking Events**: Attend job fairs, workshops, and networking events to meet new people and build connections within your industry.

2. Practice Self-Care

Prioritize self-care to maintain your physical and mental well-being. Engaging in activities that rejuvenate you can help combat feelings of discouragement.

- **Physical Activity**: Regular exercise has been shown to reduce stress and boost mood. Consider going for walks, joining a gym, or participating in yoga classes.
- **Mindfulness and Meditation**: Practices such as meditation and mindfulness can help you stay grounded and centered, reducing anxiety about the job search.
- **Engage in Hobbies**: Spend time on hobbies and activities that bring you joy. This can serve as a positive distraction and help balance the stress of job hunting.

3. Focus on Progress, Not Perfection

Recognize that the job search process is a journey, and progress may come in small increments. Celebrate your achievements, no matter how minor they may seem.

- **Track Your Accomplishments**: Keep a record of your successes, such as securing interviews, expanding your network, or improving your skills. Reflecting on these achievements can boost your confidence.
- **Set Realistic Goals**: Break down your job search into manageable tasks, such as updating your resume, applying for a certain number of jobs each week, or reaching out to contacts in your network.

4. Reframe Negative Thoughts

Challenging negative thoughts can help you build resilience and maintain a positive outlook. Recognize when negative self-talk arises and work to reframe those thoughts.

- **Practice Positive Affirmations**: Use positive affirmations to counter negative thoughts. For example, remind yourself of your skills and experiences, and acknowledge your potential.
- **Visualize Success**: Take a moment to visualize yourself succeeding in interviews and ultimately landing the job you desire. This practice can foster a positive mindset.

How to Use Rejections to Fine-Tune Your Approach

Rejections can serve as valuable feedback, helping you fine-tune your job search strategies and interview techniques. Instead of dwelling on setbacks, leverage them to enhance your future applications.

BRAVE AND PREPARED: ELEVATE YOUR INTERVIEW GAME

1. Analyze Patterns in Rejections

Keep track of the jobs you applied for and the outcomes of your interviews. Look for patterns that may emerge from your rejections.

- **Common Themes**: Identify any recurring reasons for rejection, such as a lack of specific skills or experiences. This information can help you tailor your future applications.
- **Reflect on Interview Performance**: Consider whether you consistently feel unprepared for certain types of questions or scenarios. Use this reflection to identify areas for improvement.

2. Adjust Your Application Materials

Revisit your resume and cover letter to ensure they are tailored for each application. Fine-tuning these materials can increase your chances of standing out to hiring managers.

- **Highlight Relevant Skills**: Emphasize skills and experiences that align with the job description. Use specific examples and metrics to illustrate your accomplishments.
- **Customize Your Cover Letter**: Personalize your cover letter for each application, addressing why you are specifically interested in the role and how you can contribute to the company's goals.

3. Enhance Your Interview Preparation

If you notice a pattern of rejections following interviews, it may be time to refine your interview preparation process.

- **Revisit Common Questions**: Reassess your responses to common interview questions. Practice answering them in a way that highlights your skills and experiences effectively.

- **Conduct Mock Interviews**: Arrange mock interviews with a friend or mentor to simulate the interview experience. This practice can help you build confidence and identify areas for improvement.

4. Stay Open to New Opportunities

Rejection can sometimes lead you to discover new paths and opportunities you hadn't considered before.

- **Consider Broader Job Searches**: If you consistently face rejection in a specific niche, explore related fields or roles where your skills may be transferable.
- **Be Open to Different Roles**: Consider applying for positions that may not align perfectly with your initial career goals but could provide valuable experience and skills.

5. Reassess Your Goals

Finally, use rejections as an opportunity to reassess your career goals. Are your aspirations aligned with the jobs you are applying for?

- **Reflect on Your Career Path**: Take the time to think about what you truly want in your next role. Is it a specific industry, company culture, or level of responsibility?
- **Adjust Your Approach Accordingly**: If you identify misalignment between your goals and the positions you're pursuing, adjust your strategy to align with your true aspirations.

Dealing with rejection is an integral part of the job search journey. By turning rejections into learning opportunities, seeking constructive feedback, building resilience, and using rejections to fine-tune your approach, you can transform setbacks into stepping stones toward future success. Remember, every rejection is not just an end, but a chance to grow, learn, and prepare for the right opportunity that aligns with your career aspirations. Embrace this phase of the journey, and approach it with a mindset focused on growth and improvement. With time, perseverance, and a positive outlook, you will find the role that truly fits you.

Chapter 15: Maintaining Confidence Between Interviews

The job hunt can be a challenging and emotionally taxing process. Between interviews, candidates often face feelings of uncertainty, anxiety, and self-doubt. However, maintaining confidence during this transitional period is essential for long-term success in securing a desirable position. This chapter explores strategies for practicing self-care, utilizing visualization and positive affirmations, building a robust support network, and preparing for future opportunities with renewed confidence.

Practicing Self-Care During the Job Hunt

Self-care is crucial during the job search process, as it helps maintain your mental and emotional well-being. When you prioritize self-care, you equip yourself to face challenges with resilience and optimism.

1. Physical Self-Care

Physical well-being significantly influences mental health. Taking care of your body can enhance your mood, energy levels, and overall outlook.

- **Regular Exercise**: Engaging in physical activity releases endorphins, the body's natural mood lifters. Aim for at least 30 minutes of moderate exercise most days of the week. Whether it's a brisk walk, a workout at

the gym, or a dance class, find an activity that you enjoy and incorporate it into your routine.
- **Nutritious Eating**: A balanced diet plays a vital role in your mental health. Fuel your body with a variety of fruits, vegetables, whole grains, and lean proteins. Avoid excessive caffeine and sugar, which can lead to energy crashes and mood swings.
- **Adequate Sleep**: Quality sleep is essential for cognitive function and emotional regulation. Aim for 7-9 hours of sleep each night. Establish a relaxing bedtime routine to help signal your body that it's time to wind down.

2. Mental Self-Care

Caring for your mental health is just as important as physical health, especially during stressful periods.

- **Mindfulness and Meditation**: Incorporate mindfulness practices, such as meditation or yoga, into your daily routine. These practices can reduce stress, improve focus, and promote a sense of calm. Even just a few minutes of deep breathing can help center your thoughts and alleviate anxiety.
- **Journaling**: Writing can serve as a powerful tool for self-reflection and emotional release. Spend a few minutes each day journaling about your thoughts, feelings, and experiences. This can help clarify your emotions and provide insight into your goals and motivations.
- **Limit Negative Inputs**: Be mindful of the information you consume. Limit exposure to negative news, social media, and toxic environments that drain your energy. Instead, seek out positive and uplifting content that inspires and motivates you.

CHAPTER 15: MAINTAINING CONFIDENCE BETWEEN INTERVIEWS

3. Emotional Self-Care

Maintaining emotional well-being is crucial for managing the highs and lows of the job search.

- **Practice Gratitude**: Cultivating a sense of gratitude can shift your focus from what you lack to what you have. Keep a gratitude journal and write down three things you are grateful for each day. This practice can enhance your overall outlook and boost your resilience.
- **Engage in Enjoyable Activities**: Set aside time for hobbies and activities that bring you joy and relaxation. Whether it's painting, cooking, or spending time in nature, engaging in enjoyable activities can help recharge your emotional batteries.
- **Establish Boundaries**: It's essential to create boundaries around your job search to prevent burnout. Designate specific times for job applications and interviews, and allow yourself breaks to recharge and engage in other activities.

4. Creating a Self-Care Routine

Establishing a consistent self-care routine can provide structure and stability during the uncertainty of job searching.

- **Daily Practices**: Incorporate small self-care practices into your daily routine, such as morning stretches, a nutritious breakfast, or an evening wind-down ritual.
- **Weekly Activities**: Schedule time each week for activities that promote relaxation and joy, such as a nature walk, a creative project, or a relaxing bath.
- **Monthly Check-Ins**: Set aside time each month to reflect on your self-care practices and adjust your routine as needed. This reflection can help ensure you are prioritizing your well-being.

The Power of Visualization and Positive Affirmations

Visualization and positive affirmations are powerful techniques that can enhance your confidence and mindset during the job search process. By mentally rehearsing success and reinforcing positive beliefs, you can boost your self-esteem and motivation.

1. Visualization Techniques

Visualization involves creating mental images of success, allowing you to experience the feelings and sensations associated with achieving your goals.

- **Set Clear Goals**: Begin by defining your career goals. What type of role are you seeking? What skills do you want to develop? Be specific about what you want to achieve in your job search.
- **Create a Mental Movie**: Imagine yourself successfully navigating the interview process. Visualize yourself walking into the interview room, greeting the interviewers with confidence, and responding to questions with poise. Picture yourself receiving a job offer and celebrating your achievement.
- **Engage All Senses**: When visualizing, engage all of your senses to create a vivid mental experience. Imagine the sounds, smells, and feelings associated with your success. This immersive experience can help solidify your goals in your mind.
- **Practice Regularly**: Make visualization a part of your daily routine. Spend a few minutes each morning or evening visualizing your goals and success. Consistent practice can reinforce positive beliefs and boost your confidence.

2. Positive Affirmations

Positive affirmations are statements that reinforce your self-worth and capabilities. They can help counter negative self-talk and boost your confidence during the job search.

- **Craft Your Affirmations**: Create a list of positive affirmations that resonate with you. Focus on affirmations that highlight your strengths, skills, and resilience. For example, "I am a strong candidate for the positions I seek" or "I have the skills and experience to succeed."
- **Repeat Daily**: Incorporate affirmations into your daily routine. Repeat them aloud or write them down each morning. Consider placing them where you can see them regularly, such as on your bathroom mirror or workspace.
- **Embody the Affirmations**: As you say or write your affirmations, embody the feelings associated with them. Allow yourself to feel the confidence and positivity that comes with these statements.

3. Combining Visualization and Affirmations

Integrating visualization and affirmations can amplify their effects, creating a powerful routine for building confidence.

- **Visualize While Affirming**: As you repeat your affirmations, visualize yourself successfully embodying those statements. Imagine yourself in an interview, confidently articulating your skills and qualifications.
- **Create a Vision Board**: A vision board is a visual representation of your goals and aspirations. Gather images, quotes, and symbols that resonate with your career ambitions and create a collage. Display it prominently to inspire and motivate you.

4. The Science Behind Visualization and Affirmations

Research supports the effectiveness of visualization and positive affirmations in enhancing performance and well-being.

- **Neuroscience of Visualization**: Studies show that visualization can activate the same brain regions involved in actual performance. By mentally rehearsing success, you can enhance your readiness and confidence.
- **Affirmations and Self-Perception**: Positive affirmations have been shown to improve self-esteem and reduce negative self-talk. By reinforcing positive beliefs, you can cultivate a more confident and resilient mindset.

Building a Support Network: Friends, Mentors, and Peers

Having a strong support network is vital during the job search process. Friends, mentors, and peers can provide encouragement, guidance, and valuable insights that help maintain your confidence.

1. Identifying Supportive Relationships

Evaluate your existing relationships and identify individuals who can support you during your job search. Look for those who:

- **Encourage Your Efforts**: Seek friends and family who uplift you and celebrate your achievements, no matter how small.
- **Offer Constructive Feedback**: Connect with mentors or colleagues who can provide honest feedback on your resume, cover letters, and interview techniques.
- **Share Similar Experiences**: Engage with peers who are also navigating the job market. Sharing experiences can foster camaraderie and help alleviate feelings of isolation.

CHAPTER 15: MAINTAINING CONFIDENCE BETWEEN INTERVIEWS

2. Cultivating Meaningful Connections

Building and nurturing connections is essential for creating a robust support network.

- **Schedule Regular Check-Ins**: Make time for regular catch-ups with supportive friends and mentors. This can help keep you motivated and accountable during your job search.
- **Leverage Networking Opportunities**: Attend industry events, workshops, and seminars to expand your professional network. Engaging with like-minded individuals can lead to new opportunities and insights.
- **Utilize Social Media**: Platforms like LinkedIn can be valuable for networking and staying connected with industry professionals. Share your journey, seek advice, and engage with content related to your field.

3. Finding a Mentor

Having a mentor can provide guidance and insight that accelerates your career development.

- **Seek Out Potential Mentors**: Identify individuals in your industry whose careers you admire. Reach out to them for advice or guidance, expressing your appreciation for their work.
- **Build a Mentoring Relationship**: Once you've established contact, work on building a mentoring relationship. Be open about your goals and aspirations, and don't hesitate to seek their input on your job search.
- **Offer Value in Return**: Mentoring is a two-way street. Look for ways to provide value to your mentor, whether through sharing your insights, assisting with their projects, or simply expressing gratitude for their support.

4. Sharing Your Journey

Being open about your job search journey can foster a sense of community and support.

- **Join Job Search Groups**: Look for online forums or local groups focused on job searching. These communities often share valuable resources, job leads, and encouragement.
- **Share Your Progress**: Post updates on your job search journey on social media or with your network. Sharing successes and challenges can lead to valuable connections and insights.
- **Offer Support to Others**: As you navigate your own job search, consider offering support to others in similar situations. By sharing your experiences and encouragement, you can foster a sense of camaraderie and positivity.

Preparing for Your Next Opportunity with Greater Confidence

Preparation is key to maintaining confidence between interviews. By focusing on skill development, learning, and proactive job searching, you can enhance your readiness for future opportunities.

1. Reflect on Past Interviews

Take time to reflect on your previous interviews, identifying strengths and areas for improvement.

- **What Went Well?**: Identify the aspects of your interviews where you felt confident and performed well. Celebrate these successes as they contribute to your overall skill set.
- **Areas for Growth**: Consider areas where you felt less confident or received constructive feedback. Identify steps you can take to improve in these areas before your next interview.

2. Enhancing Skills and Knowledge

Use the time between interviews to enhance your skills and expand your knowledge.

- **Online Courses**: Consider enrolling in online courses or workshops related to your field. Platforms like Coursera, LinkedIn Learning, and Udemy offer a wide range of courses that can help you build expertise.
- **Stay Updated on Industry Trends**: Subscribe to industry-related newsletters, blogs, and podcasts to stay informed about the latest trends and developments in your field. This knowledge can enhance your confidence and preparedness during interviews.
- **Develop New Skills**: Identify skills that are in demand within your target industry and work on developing them. This could include learning new software, improving your coding skills, or enhancing your public speaking abilities.

3. Networking for Opportunities

Maintain an active networking approach while searching for job opportunities.

- **Informational Interviews**: Reach out to professionals in your field for informational interviews. These conversations can provide insights into the industry and may lead to job opportunities.
- **Stay Engaged**: Regularly engage with your professional network by sharing relevant articles, commenting on posts, and reaching out to connections. Maintaining visibility can help you stay top-of-mind for potential job opportunities.
- **Attend Career Fairs**: Participate in virtual or in-person career fairs to meet recruiters and learn about open positions. These events often provide networking opportunities that can lead to interviews.

4. Setting Goals for Future Interviews

Establish clear goals for your future interviews to maintain focus and motivation.

- **Identify Target Companies**: Research and create a list of companies you would like to work for. This focused approach can help streamline your job search.
- **Set Interview Goals**: Aim to apply for a specific number of jobs each week or practice interview questions regularly. Setting achievable goals can help you stay proactive and motivated.
- **Celebrate Small Wins**: Acknowledge and celebrate small achievements, such as securing an interview, completing a course, or expanding your network. These celebrations can boost your confidence and keep you motivated during the job search process.

Maintaining confidence between interviews is a continuous process that involves self-care, visualization, building a support network, and preparing for future opportunities. By practicing self-care and employing techniques such as visualization and positive affirmations, you can cultivate a positive mindset that enhances your resilience. Building meaningful connections with friends, mentors, and peers will provide you with the encouragement and insights needed to navigate the job search journey effectively.

Ultimately, by actively preparing for your next opportunity and reflecting on your experiences, you will not only maintain your confidence but also emerge as a stronger and more capable candidate ready to excel in future interviews. The job search may be challenging, but with the right strategies and mindset, you can approach each opportunity with confidence and optimism, paving the way for your next successful career move.

Conclusion

The journey from nervousness to confidence in the context of job interviews is a transformative experience, one that many individuals undertake at various stages of their careers. Each interview represents not only a chance to showcase skills and qualifications but also an opportunity for personal growth. In this conclusion, we will reflect on your journey, embrace the notion of interviews as growth opportunities, and offer final words of encouragement as you continue on your professional path.

Your Journey from Nervous to Confident

As you navigate the world of interviews, you may find that your emotional landscape shifts dramatically. Initially, feelings of anxiety, self-doubt, and apprehension may have overshadowed your confidence. This is a common experience for many candidates, especially when facing high-stakes situations like interviews.

1. Acknowledging Your Growth

Recognizing your journey is crucial to understanding how far you've come. Each interview, whether successful or not, contributes to your growth. You have faced challenging questions, engaged with various interviewers, and adapted to different formats—each experience shaping you into a more skilled and confident candidate.

- **Reflecting on Past Interviews**: Take a moment to reflect on the interviews you've participated in. Consider how your responses have evolved, how you've learned to manage anxiety, and how you've developed your personal pitch. Each encounter has provided insights that contribute to your overall growth.
- **Celebrating Progress**: It's essential to celebrate your progress, no matter how small. Whether you nailed an answer, connected well with an interviewer, or simply felt more relaxed, acknowledge these achievements. Celebrating progress reinforces a growth mindset and motivates you to continue moving forward.

2. The Transformation Process

Transforming from a nervous candidate to a confident one requires a combination of preparation, practice, and self-compassion. Throughout this book, we have explored various strategies and techniques to aid in this transformation, such as:

- **Preparation and Research**: Understanding the importance of preparing thoroughly for interviews can drastically reduce anxiety. Knowing your material, researching the company, and practicing your pitch equips you with the tools to handle the interview process confidently.
- **Mindset Shift**: Embracing a growth mindset—viewing challenges as opportunities for learning—can change your entire perspective on interviews. Instead of perceiving them solely as evaluations of your worth, you can see them as conversations to explore mutual fit.
- **Emotional Resilience**: Building emotional resilience is a vital aspect of your journey. Acknowledging feelings of nervousness and reframing them as excitement can empower you to approach interviews with a sense of curiosity and eagerness rather than fear.

3. The Role of Self-Compassion

Self-compassion plays a significant role in your transformation. Rather than being overly critical of yourself after a challenging interview, practicing self-compassion allows you to recognize that everyone experiences setbacks. By treating yourself with kindness and understanding, you create a nurturing environment where confidence can flourish.

- **Learning from Rejection**: Rejection is often an unavoidable part of the job search process. Instead of allowing it to diminish your confidence, view it as an opportunity for learning and growth. Each rejection can provide valuable insights into areas for improvement, helping you refine your approach for future interviews.
- **Affirming Your Value**: Continually affirm your worth, skills, and abilities. Remind yourself of your achievements, qualifications, and unique strengths. This self-affirmation can serve as a powerful antidote to feelings of inadequacy, allowing you to step into interviews with confidence.

Embrace Every Interview as a Growth Opportunity

Each interview you undertake presents a unique opportunity for growth, regardless of the outcome. By reframing your perspective on interviews, you can shift from viewing them as daunting challenges to recognizing them as valuable experiences for development.

1. The Learning Mindset

Every interview can be a learning experience, offering insights into both your own skills and the dynamics of the workplace.

- **Learning from Each Experience**: After each interview, take the time to reflect on what you learned. Consider what worked well, what could

be improved, and how you felt throughout the process. Documenting these reflections can provide clarity and help you refine your approach for future interviews.
- **Seeking Feedback**: If possible, seek feedback from interviewers or peers. Constructive feedback can shed light on areas you may not have considered and provide actionable insights to enhance your performance.

2. *Building Connections*

Interviews are not solely about securing a job; they are also about building connections. Embrace the opportunity to meet new people, learn about their experiences, and expand your professional network.

- **Fostering Relationships**: Approach interviews as networking opportunities. Even if you don't secure the position, cultivating positive relationships with interviewers can lead to future opportunities. Express genuine interest in their experiences and insights, leaving a lasting impression.
- **Networking Beyond Interviews**: Beyond the interview room, actively engage with professionals in your field. Attend industry events, join networking groups, and connect with individuals on platforms like LinkedIn. These connections can lead to mentorship, collaborations, and potential job opportunities.

3. *The Journey Continues*

Remember that the journey does not end with the job offer or rejection. Each interview, whether successful or not, is a stepping stone in your career journey. Embrace the uncertainty of the process, knowing that every experience adds to your skills and confidence.

- **Lifelong Learning**: View your career as a continuous journey of learning and growth. Each role you pursue will come with new challenges and

opportunities, and your ability to navigate these experiences will only strengthen your confidence.
- **Embracing Change**: The job market is dynamic, and change is a constant. Embrace the fluidity of your career path, remaining open to new opportunities and avenues for growth. This adaptability will serve you well in both interviews and your overall career.

Final Words of Encouragement

As you conclude your journey through this book and prepare for your next interview, remember that confidence is not an innate trait but a skill that can be developed and nurtured over time. Here are some final words of encouragement to carry with you:

1. Believe in Yourself

Your confidence begins with belief in yourself. Acknowledge your unique strengths, experiences, and qualities that make you a valuable candidate. Trust in your abilities and embrace the mindset that you have much to offer potential employers.

2. Stay Positive

Positivity can be a powerful force in your journey. Surround yourself with positive influences and engage in activities that uplift your spirits. Focus on your progress, celebrate your successes, and maintain an optimistic outlook on your job search.

3. Embrace Challenges

Challenges are an inevitable part of any journey. Rather than shying away from difficult situations, embrace them as opportunities for growth. The discomfort you may feel during challenging interviews can lead to valuable lessons and ultimately enhance your confidence.

4. Be Persistent

Persistence is key in the job search process. Understand that finding the right position may take time, and setbacks are a normal part of the journey. Maintain your determination and resilience, knowing that each step brings you closer to your goals.

5. Celebrate Every Step

Lastly, celebrate every step of your journey. Whether it's securing an interview, learning something new, or simply feeling more confident, acknowledge your achievements. These celebrations reinforce a positive mindset and remind you of the progress you are making.

In conclusion, your journey from nervousness to confidence is an ongoing process filled with opportunities for growth and self-discovery. Embrace every interview as a chance to learn, connect, and evolve. Trust in your abilities, stay positive, and maintain a sense of determination as you navigate the job search landscape. With each experience, you are not only preparing for your next role but also cultivating the confidence that will serve you well throughout your career.

Remember, confidence is not just about being free of fear; it's about moving forward despite that fear. As you step into your next interview, carry with you the knowledge that you are capable, prepared, and deserving of success. Good luck on your journey—your next opportunity awaits!

www.ingramcontent.com/pod-product-compliance
Lightning Source LLC
Chambersburg PA
CBHW052208220526
45471CB00004B/1866